TRACY MILLS

21 THINGS
You Should Never Do
IN YOUR LIFE

*The
Most Controversial Book
You'll Ever Read*

21 Things You Should Never Do in Your Life
Copyright © 2023 by Tracy Mills

All rights reserved. No part of this publication may be reproduced, distributed, or transmitted in any form or by any means, including photocopying, recording, or other electronic or mechanical methods, without the prior written permission of the author, except in the case of brief quotations embodied in critical reviews and certain other non-commercial uses permitted by copyright law.

Tellwell Talent
www.tellwell.ca

ISBN
978-0-2288-8649-5 (Hardcover)
978-0-2288-8647-1 (Paperback)
978-0-2288-8648-8 (eBook)

TABLE OF CONTENTS

Controversial... v
Dedication... vii
Brief ix
Introduction... xi

Chapter 1   Be an NPC (Non-Playable Character).....1
Chapter 2   Lie to Yourself......................... 7
Chapter 3   Lie to Others.......................... 10
Chapter 4   Adopt a False Persona 14
Chapter 5   NOT Have a Personal Philosophy.......25
Chapter 6   Skip the Books........................33
Chapter 7   Skip the Podcasts 36
Chapter 8   Seek Validation on Social Media 40
Chapter 9   Swerve Hobbies 43
Chapter 10   Disrespect Your Physical Health....... 47

Intermission #1 50

Chapter 11   Disrespect Your Mental Health........52
Chapter 12   F*ck Your Finances Up 57
Chapter 13   Let Alcohol and Fast Food Control You...61
Chapter 14   Refuse to Walk Away..................68
Chapter 15   Think with Your Skin 74

Intermission #2 78

Chapter 16   Allow People to Drag You Down. 81
Chapter 17   P.R.F (Put Romance First) 85

Intermission #3 98

Chapter 18   Not Believe in Yourself 99
Chapter 19   Be Afraid to Produce Your Content . . . 102
Chapter 20   Making Excuses 108
Chapter 21   Tell People Things They Should
             Never Do 110
Chapter 22   Not Showing Love To The People! 113
Chapter 23   Leave Your Readers in the Dark 114

References 117
Book Description 119
Author Bio 121

CONTROVERSIAL

Giving rise or likely to give rise to public disagreement. Anna, you're going to be my first shout-out. I want to personally thank you for listening to me pitch my book to you. You helped me in more ways than you could imagine. Anna, if you're reading this, thank you.

DEDICATION

This book is dedicated to everyone walking on and off the beaten path. No matter where you stand in society, know that you are not alone.

BRIEF

These are my brainstorming notes.

FEEL/LAYOUT/ENERGY

Feel: I'm going to walk a fine line between kindness and tough love while questioning your character and mine.

Why do you think the way you do?
Why do I think the way I do?
Can my mistakes be used to guide someone else?
I am not perfect, and neither are you.

Layout: I'm going to make this book as simple and easy to read as possible.

Energy: I want the vibe of my book to have balanced energy. I won't swing to any side of the extremes. The extremes are:

      [Kindness/Love]   [Tough Love]

The goal is to stay in the middle, but I'll be truthful, blunt, and abrasive at times, so prepare yourselves!

I will tell my story without trashing other people. Just because I disagree with you doesn't mean I'm bashing you. Please understand that some of my descriptions won't be so pleasant, but I'll do my best not to be mean. You won't like everything I say, but I genuinely don't want to be aggressive toward you. Please bear with me. Thank you.

Listed below is a snapshot of what to expect in my book.

- I will be critical of your views.
- I will be critical of my past mistakes.
- I will challenge everything you believe in.
- There will be some cursing throughout this book.

However

- I will never insult or disrespect you.
- I will stand firm in my beliefs.
- I will encourage you.
- I will build you up.

INTRODUCTION

Why do you believe the things you believe? The more mistakes I made, the more I realized my belief system was flawed. When your foundation is decimated, you will crumble and come crashing to the ground.

Let me start by saying this:

I am not perfect. I'm a man with many flaws, and I can admit this. I have my doubts, insecurities, fears, and convictions just like anyone else. I battle with my mental health daily and I regret many of my actions from the past. However, I have a fighting spirit and I refuse to give up on myself or life.

As I sit here and ponder how I'm going to write my book, my mind constantly drifts back to the past, makes its way to the present, and boomerangs into the future. My mind is constantly going!

How will I convey what I want to say on paper? I've always wanted to write a book. For years I've been brainstorming ideas. I knew I wanted to write about my life experiences, but I just couldn't figure out how to channel that energy onto paper.

At first I wanted to do an autobiography, but then I decided to ditch that idea. That was too bland of an approach for me. After that, I thought about writing about my life lessons in the form of poetry. But then one day I was at a coffee shop writing in a guided journal, and one of the question prompts was:

"If you were to write an autobiography, what would the title of your book be?"

Out of humor, I wrote this: "Don't do the dumb shit I've done."

At first I meant it to be a joke, but as I sat and thought, I began to realize that after all these years, I finally had a solid idea for my book. I gave it a few days to stew, and then I recreated the title of my book to *52 Things You Should Never Do in Your Life.*

I began to write *52 Things* and didn't make it past the introduction before I tossed the entire notebook. I took twenty-four hours to sit and refine my idea. I didn't like my first draft of *52 Things* because I was writing out of pure anger, frustration, and bitterness. I took a day to cool off and then made it my personal goal not to write out of rage. Lastly, I decided to condense *52 Things* down to *21 Things.*

I never knew that so much energy went into creating a book. It's been a challenge to manifest my thoughts onto paper. I've thrown away many notebooks and started from scratch numerous times. But thanks to that guided journal, I officially have a topic for my book. So now it's time to share, create, produce, and ultimately encourage a new way of thinking in my readers. I'm excited to see this project come to fruition.

I want to write a "guideline" based on my experiences in life to help someone else. You don't have to listen to or do anything I say. Remember, this is my story, and only I can tell it. I'm not here to persuade or indoctrinate you. That's the media's job. I'm simply a man with a lot to say.

All I want to do is share my life successes and failures with you. If I can help just one person, then I've done my job. This will be an easy and short read.

I'm going to do my best to make sure you get the "pick it up and put it down" experience. Throughout my book, I'll break my thoughts into paragraphs to make it easier for you to engage with my content. Reading is one of my favorite hobbies. It should be fun and not a daunting task.

I have controversial and nonlinear philosophies that do not align with the narrative.

Life has hardened me, and I no longer live in fantasy or ignorance. This is your trigger warning! I see the world differently, and my stances on many topics may offend you.

With that being said, let's begin. I'm finally ready to tell my story.

Here are 21 things you should never do in your life.

CHAPTER 1

BE AN NPC (NON-PLAYABLE CHARACTER)

If you say the slightest thing outside of the programming, they will ostracize you.

I need to make this my first point because it's going to tie into my entire book. This has to be set up just right so that you won't be lost or confused. As you read on, you'll understand. But before I make my first point, I need to explain what an NPC is (for those of you who don't play video games.)

Ok, so what the heck is an NPC, and what does that have to do with me?

In video game culture, an NPC (non-playable character) is a scripted character that is controlled by the computer instead of the player. An NPC's mission is to advance the storyline of a video game by assisting the playable characters. Just think of NPCs as mindless, controlled entities whose only job is to advance the plot of the story. Meanwhile, the playable characters are controlled by *you*. NPCs don't think for themselves or make their own decisions; however, the person playing as the playable character is in complete control.

Have you ever heard the term "just going through the motions"? How many people do you know who are just mindlessly going through life as a programmed NPC? These people are empty on the inside, and it's depressing! These are the people who believe everything the media tells them. They're the ones who follow the life script down to the last detail. These people tend to always look like drained and emotionless zombies. They're miserable individuals who have allowed themselves to be programmed by whatever made them feel good.

They'll often say, "If I could go back in time, I wouldn't (insert bad life choices here)." I know you've seen them before! They all walk the same linear path, make the same linear decisions, and then complain about it. It goes a little something like this:

Go to college.
Rack up student loan debt.
Get married.
Buy a house and vehicles they can't afford.
Have kids.

Now there's nothing wrong with that path if that's what you want. But the path society tells you to take is not for everyone! What if I told you that you didn't have to take this path? Even if you're in this position right now, it's never too late to let freedom ring and take your life back. Who says you have to do those things to be happy? Society? Yeah, give me a break. At one point, society told women they couldn't vote, and there was a time when we had segregated water fountains. Society also is making all white people out to be the devil, which is ignorant and not true. People need to wake up. And this is coming from a Black man.

Just because society deemed something okay at one point doesn't mean it was right.

Just because society deems something to be okay now doesn't mean it's right.

I will make my own choices.

You don't have to be a brainless NPC who can't forge their own path.

Maybe you want to get a trade instead.
Perhaps you don't want to acquire a bunch of student loan debt.
Marriage might not be for you.
You may just want to roommate or rent/drive a budget-friendly vehicle.
Also, you might not want to have children.

You aren't a bad person if you don't follow the societal path. I'll use myself as an example. I tried to follow the NPC path, and I epically failed. Now just because I goofed doesn't mean you will. There's nothing wrong with reassessing your current position and thinking before you make major life decisions. It's almost comical how bad I tanked trying to follow what I thought a man was "supposed" to do.

I never went to college. (I joined the Marines and served from 2011–2015.)
I never got married. (I was engaged, but I tanked that.)
I *did* buy a house I couldn't afford, and it cost me bankruptcy.
And lastly, I don't see being a parent in my future.

I'm just keeping it real here. I know this seems cold, but I'm being honest. I'd rather be truthful than a liar. I told you that this book may offend you; however, this is how I feel. How I see things is neither right nor wrong. It's just my opinion and nothing else. Once again, I'm not here to convince you of anything. I'm just here to go against the grain a little bit and challenge the conventional.

So as you can see, there's a reason why I'm still single at the age of thirty with multiple failed relationships under my belt. This doesn't make me a bad person. I've just failed at many things, and the cookie-cutter lifestyle isn't for me. Now that I've figured out the NPC script isn't my destiny, things have become more peaceful!

I accepted that I've failed at some societal norms, so I started to develop a new strategy.

You must find out who you are and determine what you want in this world. You can have just as happy a life with or without marriage and kids. Don't let anyone (including family and friends) tell you otherwise. Remember, this is your one life. This is not a practice run. You won't come back again as another human, a zebra, a donkey, a tiger, a fish, a robot, or anything of that nature. Once you're dead, you are gone forever, along with all of your hopes and dreams. The cemetery is full of great ideas and inventions. Many of the dead and the living are a failure to launch. But why?

- They got comfortable with their lives.
- They are content with traveling the beaten path.
- They were too afraid to chase their dreams.

The ranch-house vision of life is not for everyone. You've been trained to believe that this is the only way you'll ever be truly happy. You were lied to.

Live your life and stop allowing yourself to be programmed!

I'm not ashamed of my failures. My failures have taught me some of my greatest life lessons.

I was an NPC for a good portion of my life. I was plugged into the matrix, and I tried to follow the linear path and failed miserably. Once I unplugged from the matrix, I started to find out who I was and began to discover myself for the first time in my life. I began to rebrand myself. I will say this: You have to decide who you want to be. You don't have to listen to or even apply what I'm telling you. I'm just simplifying stating what worked for me. However, I will challenge you to change the laws in your mind and think outside the script. You can live just as happy and successful with or without following the scripted path. It's completely up to you!

A lot of people take the NPC path and it doesn't work out. I can tell you from personal experience that buying a house and racking up a bunch of debt will not fix your relationship. NPCs are all plugged into the matrix, and they all speak the same code. Many of these people are miserable in their marriages, have bad home lives, possess ungodly amounts of debt, have disrespectful kids, battle with suicidal thoughts, and are haunted by their past failures and broken dreams.

Don't be fooled by the fancy cookie-cutter homes with the perfectly-cut, extra dark green grass, and luxury cars. Most of these people's lives are in a dismal state of affairs. The NPC path is not for everyone. You have no idea what goes on behind closed doors. Most people hate being alive, but they put on a good front for social media. Remember this, you don't have to walk the path society tells you to. You can either be a scripted NPC or a playable character. Why be a mindless non-playable character when you can just pick up the joystick of life and take control of your very own playable character?

CHAPTER 2

LIE TO YOURSELF

The worst person you can fool is yourself.

It's wrong to lie, but we all do it. I've spent most of my life lying to myself, and I still do it to this day. Every day, I have to snap myself out of being delusional and come back to reality. It's truly a struggle to be completely honest all the time.

We lie to our friends, family, spouses, children, and worst of all, ourselves. When you lie to yourself, you destroy any potential chance of growth. But why do we do it? Why would a person withhold the truth from themselves and covertly solidify their destruction?

We lie to ourselves to protect our egos from being hurt. We lie to ourselves because the truth about who we are as an individual is often ugly. We naturally want to be right, and we hate being wrong. In our eyes, we have all the answers and know what's best. We make excuses for our poor choices because it's easier to just point the finger at someone else instead of looking within ourselves and fixing the issue.

I'm guilty of all of this. Lying to myself and being disingenuous is why I've tanked so many of my friendships and relationships. How can I help you or anyone else if I can't recognize and admit my faults first?

I was an alcoholic for eleven years, but I lied to myself the entire time by asserting that I didn't have a drinking problem. Well, I did. When I quit drinking in 2021, I finally realized I was an alcoholic. I didn't know how much I drank until I stopped. I had to vocalize to the universe that I had a drinking problem, stop lying to myself, and finally break my addiction. Putting the bottle down for good was also a gateway to me breaking other addictions. Overcoming my alcoholism inspired me to stop eating fast food as well. I'm living proof that you can beat any addiction, as long as you have the *desire* to quit and stay sober. It will be the hardest thing you ever do in your life, but the pride of beating your demons is an invaluable feeling.

People often convince themselves that they're right no matter what. This is a narcissistic trait, and I'm guilty of this as well. I have extreme pride issues, and I hate being wrong. I recognize this nasty flaw in myself, and I'm working diligently to keep my pride in check. It's not an easy task, but I have a desire to be a better person. And by virtue of this desire, change is slowly starting to happen. Slowly but surely.

It's never too late to change. Every day, you can work on destroying those nasty personality traits.

So stop deceiving yourself. I challenge you all to stop fooling yourself about who you are as a person! Are you brave enough to take this journey with me?

The minute you stop lying to yourself, you immediately begin to grow!

CHAPTER 3

LIE TO OTHERS

Being completely honest all the time is very hard. Admit it—we all lie every day.

I can't stand the phrase "little white lie." A lie is a lie, period, no matter how big or small. Once you're branded as a liar, it will be hard for people to trust you. Your word is supposed to be your bond, but we manipulate and twist the truth every day.

For example, a person might tell someone, "I'm five minutes away" or "I'm almost there" when that's not true at all. Another example would be telling someone "My phone died" or "My phone's been acting up" when they simply just don't want to deal with that person.

Sometimes we lie to protect ourselves.
Sometimes we lie to protect others.

We may not want to be exposed for who we are, or we may want to avoid hurting someone's feelings. I can honestly say that I'm guilty of this myself.

I've lied to make myself look better than I am.
I've lied because I was too afraid to tell the truth about myself or someone else.

Telling the truth is the right thing to do, but the truth has consequences. Does that make it right to lie?

Are you truthful every single day? I can admit that I'm not. I know it sounds horrible on paper, but I want to be transparent here. I'm taking full responsibility and ownership of my deception. I know and understand that my behavior is corrupt.

And I refuse to justify my dishonesty.

I've burned a lot of people in my life with my falseness. I know in my heart that my character is flawed. It's not a good feeling, and I feel like scum for doing this to people. But why do we do this? Why do I do this?

We're afraid of how people may react to us being completely honest. Let's face it, we all want to be liked and accepted. Sometimes the truth is cold and hurtful. No one wants to be shunned for what they believe in, so we often twist and bend the situation to be socially accepted. I'm extremely guilty of this. I spent a good portion of my life being a chicken. I was too afraid of not being validated by other people. I was too scared to be a real man and be accountable for my actions. So I lied like a champion to the majority of people around me. This behavior is reprehensible and inexcusable. Lying to people is a disgusting thing to do, and being a dishonest snake is immoral. I've lived my entire life as a sneaky and misleading individual. I am guilty of violating good moral principles every day, and this is not the life I want for myself.

As the days go by, I strive not to lie to people but be brutally honest with my viewpoints, thoughts, and intentions. I'm not going to sit here and tell you that I'm honest *all the time*, but I'm working toward being less of a scumbag each day.

And that's a start. You don't have to be perfect.
Just be better each day that goes by.
Be a better person than what you were the previous day.

I can't sit here and tell you not to lie when I still do it myself, but hear me out. Let's be real, guys ...

We all lie. It's human nature. We want to protect ourselves and our loved ones at any cost. I'm not saying being a storyteller is right, but we all can choose to be less of a dirtbag.

No one is perfect. Perfection isn't the goal here. Gradual change is. Progress is progress, no matter how big or small. I'm not the morality police by any means. I'm not a saint or a pastor. I just want to be less of a douchebag.

We all fabricate things, but how much are you willing to destroy before you realize it's time to be more truthful? Only you can make this decision! Every day that goes by, try to lie less and be honest more. It will be a challenge at first, but as time goes on, it will become second nature.

You don't have to lie to people. I challenge you to have some integrity and reduce your deception. If you lie about the small things, then you'll lie about the big things. In the end, all you have is your word. Would you rather be seen as trustworthy or as a snake?

CHAPTER 4
ADOPT A FALSE PERSONA

Sometimes we become something we're not just to gain acceptance from people who don't even care about us.

Before we begin, I want to take you back to the Myspace days of 2008. What I'm about to write is making me cringe, but I must give you a brief background on who I was in my childhood. It's going to tie directly into creating a false persona.

I was bullied and roasted pretty bad throughout high school. I was the lame Black kid who liked anime. (For those of you who don't know, anime is Japanese animation depicting eccentric characters in their world, fighting for their causes. The causes can be good or evil, pure or corrupt.)

I stood out like a sore thumb. For starters, I was fat and unathletic. I had a big ol' Milk-Dud head with a jacked-up hairline. My clothes were baggy, and I wore those busted cheap hats with dollar signs all over them. Having a gap tooth and sasquatch feet didn't help me out much either. I was often called an "Oreo" (a Black man who is Black on the outside but White on the inside). I enunciated all of my words, and I didn't have that "cool" demeanor. I wore off-brand clothes and shoes. I got smoked for this on the regular. I had a handful of friends, but I wasn't popular at all. I struck out with every girl I spoke to, but I did manage to lock on a high school sweetheart in the eleventh grade.

Teresa, I will always love you, and I have not forgotten about you. I hope our paths cross again one day.

Overall, I was nothing in high school. I was a giant goofball and a nerd.

I was different, and at that time, I hated myself for it. I was in a nasty gridlock. I was "too White" to hang out with Black people, and I'm Black. My people wouldn't accept me, so I tried to hang out with White people, but I wasn't accepted by them either.

Back in those days, the phenomenon of a Black man "acting White" was a real struggle for a lot of us.

Where do we fit in in the world? As you can see, if you were in this predicament, it would be easy to adopt a false version of yourself just to belong. I hope things have changed since then, but this was very real back in the day. We would segregate ourselves in middle school. Black folks would migrate to the basketball blacktop, and the White folks would stay in the "picnic area" of the school yard. The pressure was on back then. That's a lot for a kid to handle. I remember being told, "Ain't you Black? Bring your ass to the blacktop tomorrow with the rest of us! And take that White boy shirt off and get you a bigger one." I remember feeling pressured to go to the basketball area just to stand there and look stupid.

Not talking to anyone.
Just standing there, being socially correct but not socially accepted.

This type of toxicity is the catalyst for a person to create a false version of themselves, no matter their skin color.

This was back in the early 2000s. I started to notice these dynamics in the eighth grade. That was a pivotal moment for me because I was starting to see how the social world worked. All I wanted to do at that time was fit in, and I was willing to do whatever it took—even go against who I was. I struggled with this well into my adult life. It wasn't until about 2019 that I finally decided to be true to myself and stop caring about fitting in. Once I did that, it set me free.

High school was a different experience for everyone. Some people loved it, and some people hated it. Unfortunately, it was a bumpy road for me, and I carried a lot of the "fitting in" mentality with me into adulthood.

I use high school as my example because a lot of us felt the pressure to belong during that phase. That pressure can cause us to morph into something we aren't. And it's not just school where we feel this! It can be at work or with our family and friends. I've battled with this my entire life. It wasn't until recently that I learned how to let that weakness inside of me go and embrace who I am as a man.

The Japanese say you have three faces. The first face you show to the world, the second face you show to your friends and family, and the third face you never show to anyone. The third is the truest reflection of who you are. Is this being a chameleon? Yes. Is this morphing? Yes. But is this adopting a false persona? No. Let's be real here, guys. You're not going to act casual and laid back at a job interview! And you wouldn't dare treat your friends like they were your boss. Would you treat your supervisor like your best friend? Would you keep it formal and professional around your close friends and family? Of course not! Different situations call for different social reactions. There's a major difference between being socially appropriate and becoming something you're not just to impress people who don't care about you.

The face you show the world will differ from what you show everyone else. Naturally, you'll be more relaxed around your friends and family. You'll be more prone to letting your guard down.

But the real you behind closed doors when no one is looking is the truest version of yourself. No one can know who you truly are unless they can go inside your mind and take up space inside your head, which is impossible. *Only you know the real you.* But let's get back to the topic at hand. I want you to ask yourself this:

Have you ever been in a social setting or situation where you weren't yourself, just to fit in with everyone else? How did you feel while doing that?

Everyone wants to be accepted.
No one wants to be ridiculed or an outcast.

To avoid that feeling of not belonging, I did some idiotic and foolish things. Looking back, it was embarrassing and pathetic. Those who seek validation from others will only destroy themselves. I am guilty of this. Don't get it twisted. I want to make it abundantly clear that I am just as jacked up as anyone else. The only thing that makes me slightly different is that I'm willing to admit that I'm a screwup and I have a desire to fight my demons. This desire to fight my demons has manifested into actions. I am a man under construction every day. Change is consistent and constant. Every day, I push to be a better version of myself than I was yesterday. It makes my skin crawl to think about how desperate for acceptance I used to be. Allow me to elaborate.

When I was in the eighth grade, I decided to adopt the "bad boy" persona just to fit in. It makes me cringe just writing this, but I am determined to tell the truth about how pitiful I used to be.

(For my female readers, the "mean girls" persona would be the equivalent of the "bad boy" persona.)

When I was in middle school, I started becoming aware of the social pecking order. It was my first time experiencing a hierarchy like this, and I desperately wanted in. I began to slowly start acting like a fool. By the time I got into high school, my cringe meter was on full blast. I wore extra baggy clothes and fake hip-hop jewelry. I'd wear my hat cocked to the side like a fake rapper, and I spent a lot of money on the newest shoes. My clothing and this phony image became my new identity. It became my obsession. I had it set in my mind to keep this facade going no matter what. I got into hip hop and rap music heavily, and I tried to morph into something I wasn't: A "bad boy."

Now I'm not blaming hip-hop for my turning into a douchelord. I blame myself for being a weak poser and trying to be something I wasn't. I chose that path. I'm not blaming urban culture for my foolish mistakes. I let that rapper image get to my head, and I started to emulate the tough guys so I could be popular too. I started acting out in class and disrespecting my teachers. I started to pick on kids who were weaker than me, and I tried to be a playboy with the ladies. I thought I was being cool by acting like an asshole, but the only person I was hurting was myself. I even changed how I walked and my speech patterns. I tried to walk like some kind of 1970s pimp, and I tried to talk like I was from a hard background. I wasn't from the streets, and there's nothing cool about being a gangster at all. Acting like a hardass was important to me, and ultimately it got me into a lot of trouble. I saw the tough guys in school and how smooth they were, so I decided to replicate what they were doing. I was just making a mockery of myself, to be honest. I was determined to keep this fake persona alive. It's sad how low I stooped to gain a "reputation."

I caught my first charge at the age of fifteen for housebreaking and larceny. Word spread like wildfire throughout my school, and I felt like I had officially become a "bad boy." I was so clueless and stupid when I was younger. I was too caught up in my selfish desires to understand the magnitude of my actions.

Actions have consequences, and I was too much of an idiot to care about how I was affecting not only myself but my family and others. It makes me cringe to think about some of the stuff I've done. But my goal for this book is to be blunt and honest. I was looking at multiple felony charges and being locked up until I was twenty-one. I brought shame, disgrace, and dishonor not only to my family but to my name as well. Luckily, I had my Dad in my corner to fight for me. He stood by my side throughout the entire legal process. I was fortunate enough to have the charges dropped on the condition that I pay two thousand dollars in restitution and serve probation until I was twenty-one. I managed to get off probation before I was eighteen, and I went off to join the Marine Corps at the age of nineteen. I'm proud to say that I've not been in trouble with the law since then, and I plan on keeping it that way!

Although my Dad and I aren't on the best terms today, I am forever grateful that he fought for my freedom and was there for me. Dad, if you're reading this, thank you.

As I moved through my adult life, I continued to allow this weakness to plague me. I was still trying to emulate something I wasn't. I was always seeking that acceptance. Thankfully, as time moved on, this became less and less. I still longed to be like the bad boy, but over time that feeling started to wear off. By my late twenties, I began to get my act together. Being accepted became less important to me, and I started to discover who I was.

My first step was to dress my age and not like a hooligan. When that happened, it encouraged me to clean my lingo up as well. Now don't get me wrong—I still love some good 'ole southern slang, but I was determined to improve my speech patterns. I expanded my vernacular and worked on speaking like a respectable adult. Dressing less aggressively and cleaning up the way I talked helped boost my confidence and improved my self-image. It took a while, but by twenty-eight, that false persona was dead and gone. I felt less anxiety around "the cool people" and I embraced being my true, authentic self. Being accepted and liked by people became an afterthought, and freedom became the only thing that mattered to me.

Forget being part of the cool crowd. There's nothing cool about being a bad boy. All the bad boys are dead, in jail, or have terrible lives. I'm not just being bitter here—I know this for a fact because I've seen it.

I can't stress this enough: Guys, never become a shill just to get the "admiration" of people who don't even care about you. Have some pride in yourself.

Looking back, it makes me sick to think that I spend the majority of my life trying to fit in and be "that dude."

I was different.
And it's okay to be different.

My older brother, Robert, told me that it's okay to be different. He told me that growing up where he's from, he *couldn't* be different. Robert, I want to thank you for sharing that with me. It's changed how I see things. Those words mean the world to me.

"Red" also showed me that it's okay to be different. I still remember the time back in 2015 when she took me to Kohls. That was my first time in that store. She showed me that it's okay for a Black man to dress outside of what is "urban" or "cool." She taught me how to set the bar much higher for myself and introduced me to Sperry's and button-down shirts. I'm thankful to her for helping me clean up my act. Some of the things Red exposed me to all those years ago are still a part of me today. She helped me step out of my comfort zone, and I am forever grateful.

I eventually learned that imitating being a hardass was a stupid idea. There is nothing cool about being a jackass. By my late twenties, those feelings of needing to belong had nearly vanished. It makes my skin crawl to think how weak my mind used to be.

But "part of maturing is royally messing up." My best friend, Douglas, told me this line and it's stuck with me ever since.

I guess I could have summed this entire chapter up by saying: "Just be yourself."

Okay, but what type of help is that? It's nonsense. Let's be real here, guys. No one likes cliche and generic advice. My goal is to connect with you, so I must make sure my voice is strong and that you can relate to me. Whether you agree with my message or not, I want my words to be powerful on paper. My views on life are unorthodox, but I don't care. I'm not like everyone else.

We're here to think, deliberate, and examine who we are as people. Someone close to me, once told me this: "Don't ever let anyone take you to the extreme where you belittle yourself and act out of being an adult. Never compromise your manhood. Don't degrade yourself."

This can apply to anyone, whether you are (or identify as) man, woman, alien, robot, trans, non-binary, gender nonconforming, ghost, donkey, or zebra. Whatever you identify as or whatever you call yourself, this can apply to you as well. No one should feel so inadequate that they start to act out of character just to fit in with people who don't even care about you.

**Yes, you need to be socially appropriate.
Sometimes just being yourself is a bad idea.**

But there is a massive difference between "reading the room" and knowing where you're at versus acting like a jackass and not being true to yourself. Remember what I said earlier: The worst person you can fool is yourself. Being delusional is a dangerous game to play. Stay true to yourself and be your real, authentic self. Don't be a fraudulent fake like I was all those years ago. Love yourself and be you.

(Yes, I know this is cliche, but at least I'm backing it with actual thoughts and events that happened in my life.)

No matter what you identify as (although I'm not really in agreement with this entire gender/pronoun thing), be yourself and stay on point. Don't become a shill for people who are just going to roast your ass to Kingdom Come. Trust me, I've been there before, and I will never, ever whore myself out again for "acceptance" and attention.

CHAPTER 5

NOT HAVE A PERSONAL PHILOSOPHY

Who are you and what do you stand for?

By definition, a personal philosophy is a set of guiding principles we live by. This is *not* to be confused with your faith. Have you ever stopped to ask yourself what your philosophy is?

Do you even have one?
And *no*, don't say, "My religion is my philosophy."
Those are two different entities.

Think of personal philosophy as an individual guideline for oneself, while a faith system is a specific set of beliefs you adhere to. A personal philosophy involves the investigation of truth, while your faith (religion) claims to be the truth but isn't based on facts or logic. If you're religious, I've probably pissed you off. I understand your frustration, but my job is to get you to think outside of your personal "truth." Remember, your "truth" is a complete lie to someone else. Just keep that in mind. If you aren't religious, we should be on the same page of music. So let me ask you this: What is your philosophy on life?

Why do you believe the things that you do?
Are you brave enough to go against your indoctrination?
Are you adventurous enough to challenge everything you've been taught?
Are you confident enough to say that your thoughts are your own?

Throughout my life, I've sold my mind to many different ideologies and philosophies that weren't my own. Sadly, I didn't realize this until 2018. Now when I try to share how dangerous this is, very few people understand. The majority of people in this world are hypnotized by being content. They have tunnel vision on the beaten path, and if you suggest another route, you'll be branded as crazy. Folks will dedicate their psyche to anything but themselves. It's sad, but this is what NPCs do. Take a look at a few things I've surrendered my consciousness to:

My parents.
My religion.
Love and romance.
The Marine Corps.
Being a correctional officer.
The NPC path, AKA The Beaten Path.

I once held all of these entities very close to me. But when you have multiple belief systems shattered in front of your face, you're forced to create a new philosophy. Your outlook on life will change when everything you once believed in gets blown to pieces.

I denounce everything I used to believe in.

I denounce being blindly loyal to my parents and family. Yes, I know this is a tough one to read, but I've learned the hard way that the people you share blood with will do you more dirty than anyone else in the world.

I denounce being blindly loyal to any religion. I grew up in the Christian faith, but I walked away in 2018. I have nothing against Christianity or any organized religion. In fact, I know some wonderful Christians who live by the faith religiously. There are two in particular whom I love with all of my heart. I can't say their names in my book, but if they're reading this, they'll know I'm talking about them. I respect these two to a high degree. They are solidified in their faith, and I've watched them walk the walk for over a decade now. They are superb examples of what it means to be a Christian. It warms my heart to know that there are still people out there with morals and Christian values.

Unfortunately for me, I've had a lot of negative experiences with "so-called" Christians. I've been hurt by them one too many times, and I'm afraid to let my guard down again. I know this is going to sound rough, but this is what I think: Some of the most hateful, vile, racist, hypocritical, and "holier than thou" people I've ever met in my life were Christians. However, some of the most down-to-earth, loving, caring, informative, and accepting people I've met were either agnostic or atheist.

I denounce giving my mind to any organization. I once sold my brain to the Marine Corps and to be a correctional officer. I was fiercely loyal to two organizations that didn't even care about me.

And I proudly denounce the beaten path. I know for a fact that being an NPC is not for everyone. You can still live a good life outside of the linear path.

People who don't have their own original thoughts make me sick to my stomach. Why believe in something just because you were taught to believe it? Who cares if your parents (or someone else) told you to live your life a certain way? I'm not telling you to become a menace to society or to be a jerk; I just want you to think for yourself. Don't go through life without questioning things. It's perfectly fine to have doubts about what you were tricked into believing. Let me ask you this: What makes a person walk away from everything they've been trained to believe? The answer is very simple: *life*.

Life has a way of shaking you to the core.

I used to see the world as it should be.
Now I see the world as it is.

You must learn how to think for yourself and develop your life philosophy. If you don't, someone else will gladly infiltrate your mind and tell you how to think. I'd like to take the time to tell you my philosophy on life and why I chose this path:

Question every ideology (even my own) and become as free as possible.

As I stated earlier, I've had many things I used to believe disintegrate in front of my eyes. This was a pivotal moment in my life, as it started my journey to truly thinking for myself. I am the most important person in my life, and I am my biggest fan. You can call me whatever you want. I don't care. I've chosen to put myself first and look out for myself first. Why? Because if I don't, who will?

No one.

I choose to live as freely as I possibly can. If what I believe in makes me immoral or selfish, so be it. I'm smart enough to know that most people don't care about you. They care about what you can do for them. Human nature is despicable. People will use you and toss you to the side like a piece of garbage—even your own family. Do you want to know a little secret on how to see if your friends and family care about you?

Ask them for a favor and see how they react.
Tell them "No" and observe how they behave.

I bet you every dime I have that when you ask someone to do something for you or tell them "no," they'll lose their minds or gaslight you into oblivion. Are you the one always reaching out to communicate? Are you the one always bending over backwards? Are you the one always putting in the effort for other people? Most people are parasites and leeches. They'll attach to you, drain you down to nothing, discard you, and find another victim. Don't believe me? Then try my experiment. *I woke up one day and decided to stop being a workhorse and a wallet for other folks.* My goals, dreams, and ambitions come before anything else. This path that I've chosen is a lonely one—I won't lie about that.

I've met some people along the way who feel the same way as me, so it's comforting to know that I'm not the only one who feels so intense about this type of outlook on life. I've been used and abused too many times. The people closest to me have done the most damage to me. I don't hate them, but I will never forgive them. Guys, I know this all sounds harsh, but many people feel the same way I do. I've grown to learn that what I do for other people will never be enough. I know you've heard the phrase: "Give 'em an inch and they'll take a mile." This phrase didn't just pop into existence by itself. There's a reason why people say it.

It's because it's the truth.

I used to make other people my purpose.
Now I am my purpose.

Instead of foolishly believing everything you've been instructed to accept as "the truth," how about you think for yourself? Remember what we discussed earlier on? You can either be an NPC or a playable character. For those of you who are part of the machine, I wish you nothing but the best. Some of us have failed miserably at the "white picket fence" ideology. Where do we fit in this world? You can't shame me into submission! I've had many people tell me my way of thinking is just an echo chamber full of sad and broken people. Well, that's true. I can't deny that at all. But my counterargument is that your white picket fence indoctrination is also an echo chamber full of sad and broken people. You're just as broken as I am. You've been molded into believing that the white picket fence lifestyle would bring you happiness. But deep down inside, you are depressed and an insufferable person to be around. You'll challenge my ideology while you secretly hate yours. You desire to free yourself.

Admit it.

You're probably just as miserable on the inside as the people who live outside of the beaten path. We all feel pain. It's what makes us human.

Some of you guys go to college, get a degree, get married, produce children, purchase a nice home, drive nice vehicles, and are still bitter, miserable, and angry individuals. So you're no better than me. Stop lying to yourself. When I stopped lying to myself, my personal life philosophy was born. I will never go back to thinking the way I used to. I'd rather be dead.

There's nothing more dangerous than a person who gaslights and manipulates someone into not having their own thoughts. If you've ever done this, you are a disgusting human being and I hope you change your evil ways! It takes a sick person to mess with someone's head.

Guys, this is your one life. I want you all to develop a personal philosophy for yourselves! I don't care who you are or what you identify as. Respect yourself and love yourself enough to figure out what you truly want out of this life. Don't let other people and the media brainwash you. Never degrade yourself to a point where you think you're not smart enough to think for yourself. I've been there before and it's such a low, sick, and sad feeling. Reclaim your mind today! I apologize if I've offended you, but sometimes everyone needs a good kick in the ass. As for me, I will never let anyone break my new life philosophy. Sure, you can challenge it, but you will never succeed in taking over my mind.

To all the broken people out there, today is the day to become a free thinker. You can do this!

To all the gaslighters out there, go check yourself!

CHAPTER 6

SKIP THE BOOKS

What's the last book you read?

Okay, everyone, let's take a quick break from the doom campaign. This one is going to be light-hearted and fun. So let me ask you this ...

What's the last book you read?
What book are you reading right now?

I believe there's no excuse for people not to read (unless they physically/mentally cannot). Nowadays, you don't even have to sit down to read! You can utilize book apps on your smartphone, such as Audible and Scribd.

Take a moment to think about your peer group.
Do you have people in your circle who suggest books to you?

My good friend Smith always shares reading material with me.

Smith, I'm proud of you, man. You've proven a lot of people wrong over the years, and I'm sorry for doubting you. Keep being the man you are and never compromise your integrity.

We live in a twisted society where everyone thinks they are "too cool" to do anything outside of drinking and partying.

Most of you guys will probably say these famous words when you're told to read a book: "Oh, I don't have time."

Come on, guys! I know we're all busy.
But you're worth the time, so invest in yourself.

You mean to tell me that you don't have five to ten minutes out of your entire day to invest in your mind? I find that hard to believe. Most folks work all day just to come home and rot in front of the TV. How in the world are people comfortable with coming home and not being productive? Work doesn't stop when you come home. It begins. You don't truly clock out until you go to bed. You have duties to your home, your romantic partner, your children, your pets, and most importantly, yourself. If the mind goes to crap, then the body goes to crap. I find it sad that people can binge-watch a TV show but refuse to dive into a book.

Some of y'all just flop right down on the couch, put your feet up, and waste away like a frog on a log. You're just throwing away your mind and stinking the place up with your feet smelling like corn nuts. Invest in yourself. Why don't you crack open a book and stimulate your mind? Feed your psyche with information and knowledge. Remember, sitting around looking crazy is not going to make you a better person. I've got a small library in my home that I've been building since 2015. I make time every day to expand my mind. Once again, if you don't like to read, there are always book apps that will read aloud to you. I know most of you guys are always on the go, but the majority of us have smartphones. Why not make the best of our technology and learn something new each day?

Remember, your mind is like your stomach. If you feed it with garbage, you will become garbage. Educate yourself and soak in information that will help you better your life. You deserve it!

CHAPTER 7

SKIP THE PODCASTS

*Legacy and social media are
a dog and pony show.*

We live in an era where limitless amounts of data are at our fingertips, and people still are ignorant. It's amazing how people use their phones for everything else besides educating themselves.

I'm a 90s baby, so I grew up in a time before the internet and smartphones. This stuff existed back then, but it just wasn't as accessible as it is today. I was born in 1991, so I got to see the world go from flip phones and CD players to smartphones and music streaming services. You'd think that with all this amazing technology, people would be on top of their game! But for most, that's not the case.

Growing up, I watched how legacy media got people to turn against one another. The classic news beef was (and still is) Fox News versus CNN. Then it slowly morphed into social media causing people to rip each other to pieces. No matter where you stand on the political spectrum, I think we all can agree that legacy and social media are absolute garbage. Most people get their news and information from social media, and that's a massive problem. However, I've noticed something over the years:

- The Baby Boomers (1946–1964) and Generation X (1965–1980) tend to flock toward legacy media.
- The Millennials (1981–1996) and Generation Z (1997–2012) tend to flock toward social media.

Can you see the problem with this? We've got the blind leading the blind. No one can think outside of the media anymore, and it's pitiful. I used to be one of those people until I discovered podcasts. I remember logging onto social media and arguing with people like a dumbass. I was immature. I allowed myself to get sucked into that vortex of drama like an idiot, but I freed myself eventually. Now I get my information elsewhere, because let's face it …

All media is corrupt and or biased.

I listen to my content creators and I stick to my podcasts. These creators are becoming so powerful, the mainstream media and social media are trying to shut them down. That should tell you something. Everyone is sick of being pandered to and lied to. That's why people are ditching streaming services like NETFLIX (they lost over 200,000 subscribers in the first quarter of 2022), not listening to the news, deleting their social media profiles, and getting their information elsewhere.

I want you to think outside of what Facebook and Instagram tell you.

I challenge you to get your information from somewhere else! The people at the top are silencing the voices of content creators and podcasters. It doesn't matter if you're on the left or the right. When it comes to legacy and social media, they lie to everyone. All they do is pander one-sided stories to everyone and pimp people out to go do their bidding. Most of you guys are pawns to the media and don't even realize it. These organizations have trained you well.

I want you to be smarter than that.

I love my content creators and I love my podcasters. I don't listen to people who push the narrative. I listen to people who challenge and question the narrative. People nowadays are so accepting of everything, Well, I'm not. I question everything, and I refuse to like and accept everything I'm told to. I will never be politically correct, and if that makes me an ass, so be it. I told you that this book would not be for the faint of heart. I don't care about being politically correct. It's not my job to give you guys a rose garden. My job is to get you to think outside of what you were trained to believe. We must be mindful of the content we consume. It's not uncommon for people to become radicalized through legacy media and social media, but some of you guys are so set in your ways, you'll always refuse to think beyond what you were instructed to believe. If this is how you get down, more power to you.

Here's what I think:

I think people hide behind race and mental health to justify their corrupt actions. Ultimately, the media uses these so-called "oppressed people" as pawns to push their agendas. Once this happens, you have a bunch of entitled people committing crimes and hiding behind these alleged racial and mental issues.

I see right through this crap. The media will spin everything they can into a racial or mental health awareness issue. **You people are out of your damn minds for falling for this same trick over and over again.**

Legacy media and social media are both brainwashing tools. These people don't care about *you*. All they care about is clicks and views. Remember, when you're out there burning, looting, and murdering in the name of "justice," these news outlets and social media tycoons are sitting at the top laughing at you fools and cashing in on the drama. Burning, looting, and murder are not done in the name of justice. These horrible acts are done in the name of chaos. Just think about that.

CHAPTER 8

SEEK VALIDATION ON SOCIAL MEDIA

*We all secretly care about
how many likes we get.*

Ok, so you just came up with the most profound status update, or you've finally taken that perfect selfie and you're ready to post it. Your thumb hovers just over the post button as you double and triple-check what you're about to share with the world. You say to yourself, "I'm so cool," and you hit the post button.

The almighty post button.

And what's that feeling in your gut that briefly follows after you've shared your masterpiece with the world?

Anxiety.
You're worried about how many likes you'll get.

You're worried about how much engagement you'll get on your content.

You posted that status or picture about five minutes ago, but you've already checked your phone fifty times. You're like a vulture circling roadkill, sweating that notification center for updates. *How many likes did I get? Who commented on my post?* Don't lie to yourself. You know you've done this before because I have! *I already told you guys not to lie to yourself in Chapter 3, so be honest.* You know for a fact that if your post doesn't go as planned, it mysteriously gets deleted.

What? I got roasted on my post, and my picture only got five likes?
Time to take this down!

I'm guilty of this, and I'm disgusted with myself for being so mentally fragile.

We all seek attention and validation on social media. Everyone wants their posts to get some love and recognition. It's just human nature. It took me years to start shaking this mentality. After some determination and practice, this mental weakness of mine slowly began to disappear. My opinion is that:

People take pictures for social media but *not* for themselves.

Why is that?
Why do we seek attention and validation on social media?

I used to be a weak man who sought online likes and approval.
Now I'm proud to say that I've freed myself of this disease.

Every picture doesn't have to be a post. It's okay to have selfies and pictures of your adventures just for you on your camera roll.

Don't determine your self-worth off of social media. Remember, people only post the highlights of their lives online. They'll make sure to post the best (filtered) photos of themselves. Don't compare your life to what you see online. Most of your friends and the influencers you follow are fake, and they post *lies* to cover up what's inside.

The summary of your life isn't measured by how many likes you get on social media. It's measured by the impact you've left on the world. Seeking validation on the internet will only contribute to the destruction of your mental health. The only validation you need is yourself. I'm my biggest fan, and I love myself. That's all the validation I need. *So love who you are* and stop worrying about how many likes you get.

And if no one has told you they love you today, I'll tell you.
I love you.
Keep your head up.
Your likes won't matter when you're dead anyway, so why stress over it?

CHAPTER 9

SWERVE HOBBIES

So what exactly do you like to do for fun?

How many of you guys have hobbies outside of work? Here's what I think:

Watching Netflix and scrolling on your phone is not a hobby.

That's just lazy, in my opinion. Most people are boring as hell and don't like doing anything outside of work. If you have hobbies, that's awesome! If you don't, go try something new! You'll never know what you may or may not like until you try it.

There was a point when I was really into archery, but it just wasn't for me. I'd always wanted to learn how to shoot a compound bow, and eventually I got one. I taught myself everything about the sport, and it was rewarding to learn a new skill. Sadly, it just wasn't my thing.

However, I do enjoy going to the firing range. My first weapon was a Glock 19, and after a few years, I traded it in for a Sig Sauer P365. The weapons range is a wonderful experience. If you've never been, I encourage you to go. As long as you're safe and knowledgeable, that's all that matters. My other hobbies are writing, reading books, and video games. (Yes, I said video games, and I'll gladly explain why in a few paragraphs.)

Journaling your thoughts is an amazing outlet and a healthy way to decompress. I find myself writing something down every day. I believe it's imperative to learn how to manifest your thoughts on paper. Instead of bitching and moaning on social media, take your thoughts and put them on paper. Social media is a disaster anyway. I find it strange that most people have a lot to say online, but they can't even write a paragraph on paper without having smoke blow out of their ears! Some of you guys are great with words and are gifted writers. The rest of you are just keyboard philosophers. I can tell you right now that crying on social media will not improve your life.

Reading books has been a part of my life since I was a kid. I mentioned earlier that I have a library in my house. I'm always reading and learning something new. There's so much knowledge out there! What's better than cracking open a new book? The satisfaction of finishing one.

And yes, I play video games. Playing Xbox is better than drinking my life away at bars and strip clubs like I used to.

We live in a society that glamorizes job burnout and glorifies being a slave (or servant) to other people. I think this way of thinking is horseshit. There's nothing wrong with being selfish. If you don't take care of yourself, no one else will. Being selfless is viewed as "morally right," but I believe self-preservation takes precedence over taking care of other people. You don't have to like what I'm saying or agree with it. It's nothing personal. I just want you to think about yourself for once.

There's no better time than the present. What's stopping you from engaging in your hobbies?

I'm going to list some common scenarios below. I hope this helps.

- Are you afraid of what your family might think?
  Don't let your family shame you into not enjoying your hobbies.

- Does your boyfriend not approve of what you'd like to do?
  Dump him. Ladies, never let a man control you.

- Does your husband not approve of what you'd like to do?
  Divorce him. If your man isn't okay with you having hobbies, then he isn't for you.

- Does your girlfriend complain about the things you enjoy doing?
  Dump her. Men, never let a woman control you. Besides, no one is stopping her from doing what she likes to do.

- Does your wife nag you about wanting to pursue your hobbies?
  Divorce her. If your hobbies bring you peace and she brings you turmoil, it's time to cut ties and move on. She's not worth it.

- Are your kids taking up all your time?
  I understand that kids are time-consuming and a pain in the ass. But you've still got to make time for yourself. Society says that your family and children are everything. I disagree. Sure, they're important, but you're important too. Always make time for yourself.

Remember, this is your one life. Do you want to be on your deathbed (or in a position where your life is flashing before your eyes) regretting not doing everything you wanted to do? Life is too short for that.

CHAPTER 10

DISRESPECT YOUR PHYSICAL HEALTH

I am not a health or mental health specialist. If you need a professional opinion, please consult with your doctor or therapist.

I can't give you medical advice in this chapter, but I will recommend/suggest that you all get established with a doctor. Guys, this is so important, and I can't stress this enough. I'm aware that not everyone can afford healthcare, and I believe that's unfair. I think we all should have the right to access affordable healthcare without it breaking the bank. As I write this in the year 2022, we are experiencing events of epic proportions.

- We are amid a pandemic.
- Inflation is through the roof.
- Gas prices are ranging from $4 to $7.

- Russia is ravaging Ukraine.
- People are quitting their jobs in record numbers.
- The housing market is a disaster.
- The automotive market is in shambles.
- People are having to choose between their health and survival.

I can fully understand some of you guys not being able to afford healthcare. Every country's economy is in a dismal state of affairs. As I stated earlier, I will not give health advice in this chapter, but what I can do is tell you what I do to stay "somewhat" healthy.

Let's just address the pink elephant in the room:

Physical fitness. I walk about ten miles a day, six days a week. This is what works for me. You don't have to train to be an Olympian; just try to be as active as you possibly can.

I'm fortunate enough to have healthcare. Yes, I understand that this is a luxury for most. If the premiums out there are too expensive for you, I encourage you to seek other avenues (*legally*) to care for your body. I utilize my healthcare plan to the fullest. I make sure to check in with my doctor every six months, and I get an annual physical. If I get sick, or something just doesn't feel right, I visit my doctor in between those semi and annual visits. Also, I use my dental and vision benefits in conjunction with my healthcare plan. As I've already stated, I know that what I'm saying is a luxury for most.

But it's your body.

It's your responsibility to care for yourself. Besides, you never know what medical illnesses you may or may not have if you don't get checked out! The sooner an issue can be spotted, the sooner it can be corrected. In addition to being physically active, I also don't drink, chew tobacco, or smoke. I don't believe in vaping, smoking weed, or the use of any other drugs (hard or recreational.) I have a zero-tolerance policy for alcohol, drunks, smoke heads, and junkies. I was an alcoholic for eleven years. There's nothing cool about drinking and smoking like a freight train. Partaking in these vices will only cause you to become addicted to whatever substance you're abusing. I believe that as long as you do your due diligence in caring for your health, you'll be fine. I know we live in an anti-doctor culture, but not every doctor and pharmacy technician are these big bad wolves the media portrays them to be.

So take care of your body. Your well-being is your responsibility.

INTERMISSION #1

A friend of mine told me this a few years ago, and it's stuck with me ever since:

"Every philosophy has holes in it."

Just because I'm writing a book doesn't mean I have everything figured out. The way I think and my outlook on life are twisted in someone else's eyes. My opinions are based on my life experiences. I am neither right nor wrong.

Most people trust what they believe in because they've been TAUGHT to or TOLD to. This includes your religion, which is something you were taught and told to believe.

For those of you still reading, I want to express my gratitude for taking the time to read my book. I can't thank you enough for giving me a chance.

For those of you who are ready to rage quit, I completely understand. My content is not suitable for everyone. I told you that my book would ruffle some feathers. No matter if you agree or disagree, I need you all to know:

My message is not a message of either love or hatred. It's a message of challenge, for I am the rare exception who would dare to challenge the conventional.

HALFWAY POINT

Ladies and gentlemen, I am happy to say we are halfway done with the show. Listed below are some questions I have for you to answer. Please feel free to be as truthful and blunt as possible. This is your time to let your voice be heard!

- How do you feel about this book so far?
- If you were to write an autobiography, what would the name of your book be?
- What is your philosophy in life?

CHAPTER 11

DISRESPECT YOUR MENTAL HEALTH

If the mind goes, the body goes.

Let's get straight to the point. We all struggle with mental health. There's a bunch of undiagnosed and untreated people out there bringing children into this world and creating more dysfunctional family units. I think this is a huge problem. We all have our highs and lows. Where we go wrong as a people is not getting the help we need. Mental health is nothing to take lightly. If you're having thoughts of suicide, please get help. I've been there before. I was ready to take my own life back in 2019, but I reached out to a suicide hotline and they talked me through it.

The year 2019 was a horrible year for me. My Grandfather died, I filed for bankruptcy, my relationship fell apart, I was having huge family issues, and I was trying to navigate the VA legal system. At that time, I felt like my entire world was collapsing, so I decided that life itself wasn't worth it anymore. This is a lot for one person to handle. It got so bad, I started actively planning to end it all. The plan was to drive somewhere secluded and shoot myself in the head. I felt so hopeless at that time, but I'm glad I didn't go through with it. I reached out to get some help, and I started to turn my life around in 2020.

Deleting yourself (I'm going to refer to suicide as "deleting yourself" because I don't want to keep typing that horrible word) is not the answer. Remember, you are not alone. If you ever get to the point where it's too much to bear, reach out to someone for help. I did, and I'm glad. Look, I know I've been a drill sergeant for most of this book, but this is a delicate situation. I can't give you medical advice, but I will tell you that if you ever get to the point of wanting to delete yourself, *please don't do it*. I've been there before, and it's such a negative place to be.

So I get it. Trust me.

If you delete yourself, you're just going to hurt the people closest to you. And if you don't have anyone, I understand that as well. But just keep this in mind:

If you delete yourself, you will never know how things would have turned out for you. Taking your life away is not an option. Listed below are a few things I do to cope each day. Maybe some of my remedies might benefit you.

- I'm in therapy.
- I don't drink alcohol.
- I don't use drugs.
- I go to bed early.
- I get up early.
- I eat three well-balanced meals a day.
- I avoid eating fast food.
- I avoid toxic people and relationships.
- I constantly stay engaged with activities and my hobbies.

What works for me may not work for you. The only advice I can give is this:

You cannot drink or drug the pain away. No matter what you're going through, doing this will not work. I promise you. I once tried to drink my pain away, and it didn't work. I'm proud to say that I am approaching my first year of sobriety. I'm so happy I got into therapy and quit drinking. Get the help you need. And if getting help and kicking bad habits causes you to lose some friends, *fuck them*. You don't need people like that in your life. Any "friend" who encourages self-destruction is not a friend at all. That person is a piece of garbage, and you're better off without them. Participating in unhealthy vices will never take your pain away. Sure, you'll forget the pain for a few hours! But when you sober up, the sadness will come rushing back. Vices only work temporarily, but therapy (which doesn't work forever) is a better route to take than substance abuse, self-harm, or deletion.

I need you to know that you are not alone, no matter how sad you may feel. Please seek help if you feel like the pressures of life are slowly suffocating you. Trust me, I've been there. I still battle with my mental health to this day. It waxes and wanes. I've been dealing with OCD (obsessive-compulsive disorder) and MDD (major depressive disorder) since I joined the Marine Corps in 2011. I went to therapy once while I was on active duty, but I didn't go back again because it's taboo to seek help while you're in the military. A lot of service members are afraid of retaliation for seeking mental help, so they just suffer in silence. Sadly, I let this sickness of mine go unchecked, and it got worse over time.

I got out of the Marine Corps in 2015, and I didn't start seeking help until 2018. I thought I was too "tough" to seek treatment, but I was wrong. There's no shame in getting therapy. Whatever you do, do not delete yourself. I know I've said throughout my book that I don't care if you agree or disagree with me on my viewpoints, but mental health is a different ball game. Now is not the time to be controversial. I want my readers to have amazing lives! I want my readers to be in good health and to be of sound mind. **I do care about your wellbeing.**

Take care of your mind, body, and spirit. This is the only trinity I believe in. You must be attentive to these three entities, for they are your lifeline. Never self-harm or delete yourself. Do not let your demons overpower you. You are stronger than that. You can do this, my friend.

CHAPTER 12

F*CK YOUR FINANCES UP

*I may not be a financial advisor,
but I'll put my two cents in.*

I've made a lot of boneheaded decisions with my finances in the past. I want to particularly focus on the bankruptcy I filed for back in 2019.

I was always irresponsible with money. I lived on a revolving checking line of credit from 2012 to 2018. Personal loans and credit cards were a major part of my life for many years. I always managed to pay my line of credit off each month ... until I couldn't. In 2017, I decided to buy a house I couldn't afford. By 2018, I was $35,000 in debt. I had maxed out my line of credit and my credit card. Racking up this debt was one of the most foolish things I've ever done. After many failed attempts at shuffling the debt around and trying to pay it off, I decided to file for bankruptcy in 2019. It took me all this to understand that charging my life away was a bad idea. I feel like an idiot for letting it get that far, but I can't blame anyone but myself. *Sometimes you have to pay for your lessons.* My goal for this chapter is to parlay my financial mistakes into a lesson for someone else.

Do not amass debt you can't pay off. I want you to consider the bullets I've listed below.

- Living on credit is a bad idea.
- Living on debit is a great idea.
- Never rack up what you can't pay off.
- It's easy to get into debt, but it's hard to get out of it.
- If you can, pay your balances off in full each month.
- Try not to carry balances over on your credit cards.

Now understand this: If you're in financial trouble, I can't save you. My mission in this book is to warn people not to make the same mistakes I did. I can only help those who want to be helped. And if you don't want my help, I respect that. **You don't have to listen to me, but you're going to listen to your bill collectors. That's for damn sure.** These guys have successfully tricked *us all* into being debt slaves. These companies want you to pay the minimum so that they can pile interest on you. I want you guys to *think* before you destroy your finances. That one swipe at Ulta or Academy Sports can potentially set you back for three to six months. Do you think it's smart to be financing groceries and dining out? What type of return can you get on that? We live in a culture where people glorify financing everything. I can tell you right now that by financing everything, you will slowly bleed your account out every time you get paid.

Bankruptcy ruined my credit, and this is going to be on my credit report for the next seven years. I don't encourage filing, but if you have to, so be it. It's been about three years now, and I'm slowly rebuilding my credit score. I make sure to pay my credit card balances in full each month, and *I refuse to live on credit.* I have a strict budget and I stick to it. I save money by eating at home, packing a lunch for work, and not consuming alcohol. Eliminating fast food and alcohol nets me an extra $500 a month in my budget. I want you to stop and think about your budget.

How many of you are just eating and drinking your paycheck away? You'd be surprised how much money you blow on booze and eating out. A bonus for me in tightening up my finances is that I lost twenty pounds. Make cuts and sacrifices where you can. You don't have to go out every weekend. Sometimes you might have to sit at home and find other ways to entertain yourself. Do you want to be that guy/gal who gets paid on Friday and is broke by Monday?

YIKES.
That used to be me.

I was the moron who partied and ate my check away. I used to piss my money away on nonsense.

Not anymore.

I only buy what I need, and I keep my wants under control. Sure, I treat myself from time to time. But these bills come first! Also, I don't mind staying at home and being responsible. I used to be the guy at the club, burning my money on strippers and drinking like a madman at the bar. Now I'm the guy staying at home, reading and writing books on the weekend. I'm staying out of trouble and keeping my bank account intact.

The streets used to be my purpose.
Now my dreams are my purpose.

You want your checking account to be so strong that you're carrying over money into the next payday. Tighten up your finances before it's too late. If you're in a bad situation, it's time to consult with a lawyer. But if you can save yourself before it's too late, then make it happen!

Your wallet and your waist will thank you. Keep this in mind:

If you disrespect credit, it's going to disrespect you.

As I stated earlier, you don't have to listen to me, but you will listen to your bill collectors.

CHAPTER 13

LET ALCOHOL AND FAST FOOD CONTROL YOU

Whenever I see people drinking their lives away and consuming fast food, I think of these individuals as slaves.

We are all slaves to something.

Every last one of us is in bondage to something, whether it be to your job, kids, husband, wife, or even your family. You're all being held in some form of captivity, including myself—especially those of you with vices. In 2019, I set out on a journey to make myself as free as possible. One day I woke up and said: "I'm tired of being pathetic." Then I decided to rid myself of alcohol and fast food forever.

I'm tired of being pathetic.
I'm not where I want to be in life as a man.

I had to challenge my character to become a better man. I was sick of being a loser, so I adopted a no-nonsense attitude and began to slowly implement changes in my life.

"Fuck being weak. This is my life. Take control and stop making excuses."

I tell myself this every day, and you should do the same! Your excuses mean absolutely nothing to me. It's time to take action. There's no time better than the present!

I'm going to break this chapter down into two parts and briefly discuss how I overcame these two vices.

Beating my addiction to alcohol:

As I've stated throughout this book, I was an alcoholic for eleven years. I picked up this habit while I was enlisted in the Marines Corps (2011–2015.) My alcoholism was not the military's fault. *No one forced me to drink. I did it to myself.* For the past eleven years, I used alcohol as a coping mechanism. People would have described me as a "happy drunk." It was euphoric for me when I drank, and I made a lot of poor choices as a result of this. For years I wasted money at the bars, made a mockery of myself in front of women, threw cash at strip clubs, and put my life in danger, all for the sake of "having fun." Beer was my drink of choice, and I drank about four to six times a week. It was never one or two drinks either. I could easily crush a six-pack and report to work the next day like nothing ever happened.

My drinking intensified when I became a correctional officer. I had a serious drinking problem and I couldn't see it. A few people tried to warn me, but it fell on deaf ears. The final straw for me was when I made a complete spectacle of myself at a Fourth of July party in 2020. I embarrassed the hell out of myself by acting like a medieval-period court jester. I was the talk of the town for a while afterwards, and no one has forgotten it. **This is the cycle I enslaved myself to:**

- Get drunk.
- Act a fool.
- Hangover.
- Repeat.

In 2021, I quit drinking altogether.

As of today (May 30, 2022), I have been sober for one year. It was hard at first, and I almost relapsed a few times, but I stuck with it! I was determined not to be a drunk anymore, and I made it happen. I can't tell you how many cans of sparkling water I drank when I first quit. I had to find a creative way of simulating coming home and cracking open a cold one. I successfully tricked my mind into thinking I was drinking without actually drinking. I reprogrammed my brain to feel the satisfaction of having a cold beer after work with sparkling water as a substitute. I know this sounds crazy, but it worked.

I also use a sobriety-tracking app to help me along my journey. Each day, the app prompts me to take a pledge to stay clean. Once I make my pledge, I go through my day as normal. When it's close to bedtime, I log my progress, notes, and feelings for that day in the app, and it keeps track of my sobriety streak. I'm living proof that you can beat any addiction. You just have to be willing to make the sacrifice and fight for what you want. You can quit drinking today if you truly want to. It will probably be the hardest thing you'll ever do, but it can be done.

I used to think I couldn't live without alcohol.
Now I don't feel that way anymore.

I've defeated one of my greatest demons, and words alone can't express the pride I feel over this accomplishment.

Beating my addiction to fast food:

How many times a week do you visit the drive-through?
What's your favorite fast-food spot to eat at?
What's your favorite thing on the menu?

Some of us have been putting this garbage into our bodies for years. I know I have. I remember hitting the drive-through two to three times a day, multiple times a week. I can still remember the sluggish and disgusting way fast food made me feel. It made me feel like crap, and my left arm would tingle after eating this trash. One day I woke up and said:

"If I can quit drinking, I can quit fast food."

The first step was reducing my fast-food intake to twice a week, then once a week. Eventually I cut the drive-through out of my life completely. Cutting fast food out indefinitely was harder than quitting drinking. Fast food is delicious and convenient. This is why so many people struggle with letting it go. Because I gave up alcohol, it inspired me to stop eating fast food.

Quitting alcohol was the catalyst for quitting fast food.

I was 245 pounds in 2021, and now I'm down to 224.

If you're struggling with an addiction, I hope my story can help you overcome your vices. Don't be a slave to whatever is holding you back. Most of us let booze and fast food control our lives. You're better than this!

Enablers, companies, and corporations want you to be overweight, drunk, and ignorant.

- If you're overweight, people will *enable* your poor eating choices when they *know* it's unhealthy. They'll say it's "body shaming" to judge someone based on their appearance. I believe that you should be judged on how you present yourself to the world. Remember, how you carry yourself is a direct reflection of you!

- If you're a drunk, the only people who will benefit from this will be the bars and the alcohol industry. These people don't care about you. They want you to drink so that they can line their pockets up with your money.
- If you're ignorant, you will *refuse* to think outside of fast food and alcohol culture. You will continue dumping garbage into your body, slowly killing yourself over time. This is *exactly* what these companies and corporations want. Sadly, some of you are too blind to see this.

In addition to this, you have the media encouraging "body positivity." There's nothing positive about being overweight. You've been conditioned to believe that your body is perfect no matter what shape it is. I call bullshit on this. Now is the time to re-examine how you go about carrying yourself. Try cutting these two things out and watch what happens to your body!

Does your drinking control you, or do you control it? Can you imagine a life without fast food?

I was once a slave to these two forces of darkness. But now I am free.

I was once called "pathetic" by someone close to me for my drinking, and it's stuck with me ever since. Once you get called a name like that, you'll remember it until you die. That was one of the many reasons why I decided to walk away from drinking and consuming garbage.

I won't mention her name, but you know exactly who you are.

Red, thank you for those cold but caring words. It was you who ignited the spark in me to start changing for the better.

Your life is worth so much more than an eight-ounce can of booze and a fast-food burger. Instant gratification may feel good at the moment, but it will destroy you in the long run.

Make today the day you walk away from alcohol and the drive-through.

Officer Cooper, I'd like to thank you as well. You probably don't remember me, but I remember you. You told me something back in 2015 that I will never forget. It was this:

"You're stronger than an eight-ounce can."

I'll never forget those words. Thank you for trying to help me with my drinking problem. I didn't listen to you all those years ago, and I'm sorry. I've applied your wisdom to my life, and now I'm ready to start giving back through my content. Peace and blessings to you, my brother.

CHAPTER 14

REFUSE TO WALK AWAY

*I'd rather be alone than be
surrounded by people who are
going to disrespect me.*

Out of respect for the people involved in my situation, I won't name-drop. I'm going to tell my side of the story to the best of my abilities without dragging other people's names through the mud.

I want you all to take a minute to think about this question I'm going to ask you:

Who has crushed your spirit the most in life?

Sometimes it's the ones closest to us who hurt us the most. Your family, friends, and romantic partners will destroy you in more ways than you can imagine. These people will gaslight, manipulate, use, and abuse us. Yet we allow them to stay in our lives because we view them as "family." This trinity will decimate your mind, body, and spirit if you allow them to, and they won't give a damn about how you feel.

Your Friends:

Let's get straight to the point. Your so-called friends are more like acquaintances. These people will smile in your face and stab you in the back. I want you to take the time to examine your friends. Are these people really in your corner? Can you depend on them in your time of need? Just recently, a friend of mine had $750 stolen from his bank account. All his friends bailed on him in his time of need, but I was there for him. I gladly sent him $20 and reassured him that if he needed anything, I'd be there for him. *If I was down and out, I'd want a friend like me.* If your friends aren't willing to have your back when you need them the most, it's time for you to walk away. I'm not saying that your friends should have your back in *every* situation, like if you want to do something detrimental to your wellbeing. Being a true friend doesn't mean that a person co-signs everything you do. Sometimes your friends *need* to check and correct you! What I'm saying is that if your friends are freeloaders and all they do is take, it's time to remove them from your life. Only you can make that decision, though.

Your Family:

They say that "blood is thicker than water." I say that's *not* necessarily true. I don't think blood is thicker than water. Your family will break you faster than anyone else.

Sometimes a stranger will show you more love than your blood.

How many of you have been burned by your family but you tolerate it because you're related? Do you feel like a child around your parents, or do you feel like an adult? Can you proudly express your thoughts and opinions without being anxious around them? Are you allowed to be yourself without worrying about what they'll think? Do you want to be yourself or the person you were raised to be?

There's no shame in deviating from what you were taught to be. Your family doesn't always have your best interests in mind.

- What if you were taught to only date a certain race?
- What if you were told that you could only date the opposite sex?
- What if you were instructed to follow only *one* particular religion?
- What if they want to be Grandparents but you don't want kids?

If you were to become the person you've always wanted to be today, would your family disown you? What type of person would disown someone just because they don't think like them? How many of you out there are afraid to embrace being yourself because you're terrified of what your family might think or say? Are you willing to sacrifice what you want for the sake of your bloodline, or do you want to stay true to yourself? I need you to ask yourself this question:

What's more important to you, your family or your freedom?

At some point, you'll have to make that decision, and it will be one of the hardest choices you'll ever make.

In 2019, I decided to walk away from my parents. I had a major disagreement with my Father back in 2018, which resulted in me choosing to go no contact. **I want to make it clear that I chose estrangement, and I'll explain why.** We got into an argument that got out of hand. In this situation, everyone is at fault. It could have been handled a lot better, but it didn't happen. I'm not here to claim victim status. I'm just as guilty as my parents (even though they'll never admit their role in this). Walking away from your parents doesn't happen overnight. Usually, a person cuts someone off after years of animosity building up. Then it only takes the smallest incident to cause a verbal altercation. Ultimately, this may lead to estrangement.

The nail in the coffin for me were the two things listed below:

- They refused to reconcile with me after many people tried to get them to (including myself).
- They did a smear campaign on me.

These two acts are unforgivable in my eyes. If you have time to do a smear campaign, then you have time to reconcile.

I want you to ask yourself this:

Would you put up with disrespect from these people if they weren't your family?

No, of course you wouldn't! You'd tell them off in a heartbeat, but because these folks are your family, you hold back and tolerate the abuse.

I will always honor my Mother and Father, but I will never forgive them or forget what they did to me. I will always stand up for myself, even if it's against my family. I understand that I'm not perfect and I wasn't the best son to my parents; however, I paid it forward when I moved out at nineteen and joined the Marines. I will never bad mouth my parents as they did to me. At this point, I'm just going to continue moving forward in life, with or without my family.

If you're in a situation where it's unbearable to be around your family, wash your hands and walk away. You're not a bad person for choosing yourself. Sometimes it's the ones closest to us who will burn us the most. I know this is a hard pill to swallow, but your mental health, wellbeing, and peace are more important than your family. Blood is not thicker than water, and family is not everything.

Your Romantic Partners:

People will stay in toxic relationships just to avoid being alone. In Chapter 17, I'm going to dive deeper into this. Believe it or not, most of you are sleeping with the enemy and don't even realize it. Be wary of the partner who "loves hard." If they can love you "unconditionally," then what are they capable of when you two split up? If they can swing to one side of the extreme, they can swing to the other side as well.

Those who go hard for you during the relationship will go hard against you when the partnership ends.

Don't let the fear of being alone cause you to stay in a terrible relationship. When something doesn't add up, start subtracting!

In Chapter 17, I'm going to dismantle the idea of romance and "unconditional love." Until then, kick back and enjoy the ride.

CHAPTER 15

THINK WITH YOUR SKIN

*My ethnicity doesn't control
how I make decisions.*

I'm not too sure how I want to approach this chapter. Honestly, I'll admit that attacking this topic will be tough. As I've navigated through life, I've noticed that people will box themselves into certain ideas and ways of thinking based on their skin color. I think this is a bad move. I understand that different races have different cultures, but I choose to see right through race-baiting nonsense. This subject is not going to be easy to write about, but I'll do my best to convey my message. I've observed that the majority of people think like this:

- "I'm Black, so I have to do these certain acts and agree with this or that."
- "I'm White, so I have to do these certain acts and agree with this or that."

I honestly believe that most people are brainwashed into moving through life in a particular way because someone told them to. Most of you were probably told to "beware of the other race." I understand that people of all shades will experience life differently, but we can't allow ourselves to think with our skin. **No matter what color you are, be proud of your heritage.**

White people, that goes for you too. I'm fully aware that the media is demonizing your people, and I don't think that's right. We all (no matter what color we are) have the right to be proud of our bloodline and our ancestors. Take pride in who you are, but never think with your skin. Making that choice won't be easy, and it will come with consequences ...

But you will grow.

People make irrational decisions thinking with their skin and not their brain. I equate thinking with your ethnicity instead of your mind to thinking with raw emotions instead of logic.

I'll use myself as an example. I'm Black, but I lean toward the right. I'm not big on labeling myself, but I hold mostly conservative views. Unfortunately, I'm viewed as a "sell-out" in my community. Why? Because a lot of my people think with their skin. If they'd try to get to know me, they'd find out that I rock with plenty of people on the left. I agree and disagree with things on both sides. Just because I lean toward the right doesn't mean I'm a bad person. This way of thinking is destructive and dangerous to us all. Just because I'm a Black man doesn't mean I have to align myself with certain movements and political ideologies. I will never allow my skin color to dictate what I believe!

These corrupt bastards will never control me. I was born hard-headed, and that will never change. I will always think for myself, and I will never back down from my position.

The people at the top want us to be divided so that they can conquer us. Once you get people to think with their skin color, the damage has been done. They'll turn against one another and destroy each other. Some folks will never think outside of their race, and it's sad. The elites have succeeded in the destruction of our society. For everyone who has participated in this madness, shame on you. You were played like a fiddle and you don't even realize it.

**My skin color doesn't define me.
I define myself.**

Don't let someone else poison you into thinking that you have to be a certain way just because you look the way you do.

To all the covert freethinkers out there, I understand your pain. Keep fighting for what you believe in.

To all the overt, loudmouth race-baiters out there, shame on you. It's people like you who are the problem, not the freethinking normal people who just want to live a happy life.

INTERMISSION #2

These are the stages of becoming a free thinker.

1. Believing everything people say.
2. Noticing their inconsistencies.
3. Understanding that people lie all the time.
4. Finding humor in their pitiful attempts to manipulate you.

I've noticed that people will call anything "hate speech" if it goes against the popular narrative. Disagreeing with something is *not* hate speech. In today's world, you're not allowed to have your own opinion if it isn't the "right" one. Having a different opinion will get you branded as an "ist," "ism," or "phobic." If you don't fit the "right" side of the agenda, you can be subjected to vigilante justice. There are people out there who will cancel someone just for having their own opinions. I've noticed that these beasts tend to target and bully the individuals listed below:

- Straight people.
- Religious people.
- White conservatives.
- Black conservatives.

Although I don't align myself with any political parties, I hold mostly conservative values. This within itself has been demonized in today's society. There are some protected groups out there that can instigate and antagonize others that don't conform to their agendas. I need to make this clear:

I'm not on anyone's side. The only side I'm on is my side.

I believe both the left and the right are just as equally corrupt, but I can say with confidence that the right is the lesser of two evils. I know that comment may piss some of you off, but you'll be fine. Unlike some of you, the media doesn't influence me. I see deception in both political parties. At the end of the day, we're all just another vote. No matter where you stand, be sure to remember the bullets listed below:

- It's not your job to shun religious, conservative, straight people.
- It's not your job to shun non-religious, liberal, (insert sexuality here) people.

The only people you should shun are the monsters who hide behind their narratives and persecute others.

I want you to listen to what I'm about to say:

I will always think for myself. I'm done giving my loyalty away to just anyone and anything.

What's more important to you? Your thoughts being your *own* and people not liking you, or your thoughts *not* being your own and people liking you?

Only you can decide.

THE DEVIL'S ADVOCATE

1. A person who expresses a contentious opinion to provoke debate or test the strength of the opposing arguments.
2. A person who advocates an opposing or unpopular cause for the sake of argument or to expose it through contamination.

People want you to pick a side so that they can either "love" you or hate you. But if you refuse to pick a side, they will hate you the most. Stay away from people like this. They are bottom feeders and the lowest common denominator of a human being.

CHAPTER 16

ALLOW PEOPLE TO DRAG YOU DOWN

Never let anyone undermine your success!

Progress is progress, no matter how big or small. Unfortunately, there will always be a troll ready to cut you down. As you begin to climb your way to the top, you'll encounter some insecure dickheads who will try to drag you back down into the abyss. When I was younger, I used to feel guilty for putting others on the back burner and focusing on my goals. Because of this guilt, I almost gave up on my dreams a couple of times. I was a feeble man just a few years ago. Now I'm stronger than ever and I've overcome these mental roadblocks.

In this life, you will run into **dream killers** who will attempt to sabotage you and your plans to succeed.

Do not feed into these people.
Do not let them derail your life.

If you allow them to, they will change the trajectory of your life. Dream killers are nothing more than losers with a bunch of excuses. These people usually hate themselves, haven't accomplished a damn thing in their lives, and are jealous of others who became something. Dream killers will use every tactic in the book to make you feel bad about bettering yourself. Don't listen to these assholes. They are the scum of the Earth.

There are people out there who will tear you down just because you want to improve your life. Beware of your family and friends. Some of your worst enemies will be in your social circle. This includes the person you share a bed with. I know I'm coming off as harsh, but the reality isn't always sunshine and rainbows.

Never let anyone convince you to forsake your destiny. Sometimes you have to put everyone on the back burner and focus on yourself. If your life isn't together, how can you lead and guide someone else? Always remember that your ambitions come first.

I've noticed that as you start to ascend, you'll face some opposition. It's rather bizarre, but here is what I've discovered:

- If you are a bum, you will be branded as a loser.
- If you accomplish things and begin to gain confidence in yourself, your efforts will be minimized and reduced to "showing potatoes." People will eventually start to exit your life out of jealousy, and they'll brand you as a loser.

So it doesn't matter how much ass you kick. Someone will always shit on you and every milestone of your journey. It's almost like the bird that always takes a dump on your car. No matter what technique you employ to keep your car dookie free, some bird will always find a way to crap on it. This analogy ties directly into the real world. You can be killing it in life, and someone will still find a way to defecate on you. I don't give sub-humans like this the time of day. All they're going to do is roast people who are making something of themselves and go cry on Reddit. That's exactly what these bottom feeders do. Never let the scourge of the Earth drag you back into the pit. *You are so much better than them.* Negative creatures like this get eliminated from my life and flushed down the toilet like a used piece of tissue paper. Forget them. If you don't take anything else from this chapter, I want you to remember this:

You are worth so much more than you realize. Never let the dream killers bring you down. Your achievements matter and so do you.

To all the crabs out there trying to escape the barrel, keep climbing to the top. You can do it!

Never let anyone else drag you back into the darkness.

To all the dream killers out there, shame on you. Stop trying to discredit someone else's success just because you've failed!

CHAPTER 17

P.R.F (PUT ROMANCE FIRST)

I believe unconditional romantic love is a myth.

In my opinion, hopeless romantics are some of the most delusional and destructive people on the planet.

These people have failed in every relationship they've been in, and they have the nerve to counsel others on love. I can admit that I've bombed all my relationships as well. However, I would never preach the gospel of romance to you guys. You see, there's a difference between them and me.

- The hopeless romantics are failures at love trying to lead you back to relationships. They want you to put others first.
- I'm a failure at love trying to lead you back to freedom. I want you to put yourself first.

I honestly believe that people have attachment issues. I also believe that people are in love with being in love! That's why the divorce rate in America is so high. Fifty percent of all marriages in the United States end in divorce or separation. So that means half of marriages will fail, and the other half "work out." I can guarantee you that the "successful" fifty percent are staying together for other reasons besides love, but I'll save that argument for another time. In my entire life, I've only seen one truly successful marriage. I won't mention their names, but these two people are very close to me, and I respect them for who they are and what they represent. They are the rare exception to the rule. Other than them, the rest of these people out here are like a bull in a china shop when it comes to love. They're terrible at it. We've got way too many people making romance a priority when they're a hot mess. Okay, so let's get back to the topic at hand. I want to focus on romance once again. Let me ask you this:

If romance is so great, why does it fail half the time?

I know exactly why.

People are in love with new love. They're addicted to the adrenaline rush of dating someone new. They like the butterflies they get from the honeymoon phase of the relationship. If this is you, I have to call you out on it. You're out of your mind. When someone in the relationship stops getting the attention and validation they used to get, they'll go and seek it from someone else.

(Eighty percent of all divorces in the United States are initiated by women.)

Now let me say this:

Life happens sometimes.

A man might not be able to focus the usual attention on his woman. He may be going through a situation that saps him of all of his strength, and he may be internalizing his pain. He may not want to come to confide in you for everything. He's supposed to be the rock, and the weight of the world is on his shoulders. Being a provider isn't as easy as it looks. But if you think you can do it better than a man, prove me wrong. Anyway, as I was saying, if that energy from the man slows down and she's not getting the usual validation, she'll seek the attention from someone else and claim that you "abandoned" her. I know this from personal experience. I personally think that:

- Unconditional love (family, friends) is real. These bonds can be broken, but you'll always love your kin and your people no matter what.
- Unconditional romantic love is a farce. People swap out relationships like they do iPhones. If this type of love existed, then why does it end once the couple breaks up?

These are the hard questions people are too afraid to ask. They're scared of how people may view them for thinking like this. Luckily for you guys, I'm the *man* who asks and says everything you aren't allowed to. I want to take a closer look at the people who crusade the hardest for romantic love.

Let's start with these individuals first. There are a lot of broken people out there looking to complete themselves by attaching to someone else. I view this as pathetic and weak. These people are not only a danger to themselves but a danger to others. They usually have no hobbies, dreams, or ambitions, and their relationships usually come to an absolute toxic end. These people value relationships above all else (including themselves) and will nuke everything around them on their quests for love.

NOTE: I said quests for love because these people go from one relationship to another with less than six months in between. They will never learn.

Some of the most broken people will try to school you up on love. These people have a deplorable relationship track record, but they know everything about making a union last! This is pure delusion and it's an insult to my intelligence to even entertain these types of people. Some of you guys need to leave the alcohol, pills, drugs, and fast food alone. It's affecting your ability to think straight. You truly cannot fix stupid.

There's no such thing as "love conquers all" in today's world.

You will only be loved if you don't violate the terms of the relationship.

But if you do violate the terms (no matter how big or small), the love they had for you will vanish. Don't believe me? Piss your partner off to the point of no return and watch what happens. Let's take a look at this list I've created. If at any point one (or multiple) parts of this list are compromised, the relationship is doomed to fail. Why put romance first when it takes so little for that intense love to disappear and morph into disdain?

RESOURCES

ENERGY

ATTENTION

TIME

FIDELITY

I call this bad boy R.E.A.T.F., and I'm going to break down each component of this to drive my point home. **There's no such thing as unconditional romantic love.** The person you sleep next to at night will destroy you if you push them too far. Sometimes your biggest enemy is the person you share a bed with. Some people may call me cynical, but I say fuck what they think. I'm just a realist telling his story. Half of you guys reading right now are terrible at love, and you should be putting yourself first.

Some of you are so hurt on the inside that you dislike yourself.

How can you love someone else when you don't even love yourself?

Resources

Finances are one of the top reasons why relationships fall apart. Nothing can terminate a relationship faster than someone who is not financially responsible (except for infidelity). I learned this the hard way. When my economic status started to deteriorate back in 2019, it severely impacted my relationship. I'd say that was the nail in the coffin for my engagement being called off.

I can admit that I was no saint before the engagement was called off, and I'm not here to put all the blame on her.

If you can't provide or pull your weight, that "unconditional love" will start to dissipate and your partner will seek financial security from someone else.

Energy

Energy equals Effort.
(E.E.E.) (Triple E)

You need to remember this acronym I've created. You must expend energy to maintain a partnership. Sadly, energy is not free.

So what do you do when you want time alone but your significant other wants to be around you? What if your energy and effort aren't enough for them? The person you love could be insatiable, so how do you satisfy them? Everything you do in a relationship requires energy. If you aren't careful, they'll use up all of their energy and start feeding on yours. When you don't have any more to give, they won't have any more love to give.

Attention

I can honestly say that I love attention, especially from females. So I would be a hypocrite to be critical of this subject without calling myself out on it first. The best person to call out bullshit is a person who does bullshit. And since I love female validation so much, I can speak on the flaws of desiring attention.

Some people can't function without the attention of others. I used to be bad about this, but I've gotten my thirst under control. I'm in a position where I can solely focus on myself, and I love it. I don't need the attention of other people because I understand they'll replace me without a moment's hesitation.

Trust me on this one. I'm going through it right now as I type this out.

But what about the people who thrive on attention in relationships?

These people can't be pleased with the attention you give them because they'll always crave more and more. If you dip below what you normally supply, they'll begin to find it in other places. What if you have a situation that rocks you to your core and you have to focus everything on fixing one or multiple issues? Is it wrong to put your lover on the back burner and zone in on your issues?

Yes, it is.

But that doesn't stop people from doing it. Financial issues, family issues, legal issues, and death are a lot for one person to handle. Yes, you should talk to the person you love about your problems. But where's the line you draw on what you can and can't tell them? Would they ever get tired of listening to you?

What about the people who choose to internalize their issues? As I've said before, hopeless romantics (failures at relationships) tend to know everything about making love work, but they can't logically answer these questions. They move out of emotion. I move out of logic. This is why I've walked away from romantic love as a whole. You cannot reason with an emotional person.

Is internalizing your pain a healthy way to cope?
Of course not!

But is running your lover down with your issues a healthy way of doing things?
No!

When is it too much and when is it not enough? I don't have to make those decisions anymore, because I've chosen to live for myself. These are the questions you must consider. I'm a failure at love. There's no question about it. But I was smart enough to take myself out of the dating world and heal because I don't have all the answers. It's the hopeless romantics who seem to know everything about love, but they've never had a successful relationship in their lives. Time together is not a measure of success. If you've broken up or divorced, you're a failure at love. I know it sounds harsh, but it's the truth. You are only a success if you stay with that person forever. **That's what monogamy is.**

I will say this. If something is bothering you on the inside, talk to the person you love. You don't have to suffer in silence as I did. I chose to be Superman, and it cost me dearly. When you break up or divorce, you lose everyone around you associated with that union. It's the death of you, your lover, their family, and yours. When that relationship comes to an end, it has a domino effect. Everyone is affected, and years' worth of friendship comes to a screeching halt. In some ways, a breakup or divorce can be equated to dealing with the death of a loved one.

If you decide to focus solely on survival while in a relationship, it will be detrimental to the union and there will be no coming back from that. Trust me on this one. I'm currently navigating through this anguish right now.

That unconditional love will disappear faster than toilet paper did back in 2020. If you violate the condition that is attention (it doesn't matter what you're going through), you will be branded as "neglectful," and that person will go seek validation from somewhere else. It's a cold world out there. I once read a story about a young man who lost his Mother. He became very depressed, and his girlfriend couldn't handle it. So she left him, just like that. Guys, you better listen to the words I'm telling you. Your worst enemy is the person who claims to love you unconditionally. Romantic love is one of the most volatile and fragile things I've ever seen in my life. That person may look sweet and innocent, but they will obliterate you once the relationship comes to an end. I'm experiencing this right now. Listen to what I'm saying and be wary of jumping into romance so quickly. If you deviate from the attention you were previously giving out, they will find it in someone new. The sad thing is, these hopeless romantics don't give a damn about what you're going through. They're all like drug addicts. If they don't get your attention from you, they'll go get it somewhere else. These people remind me of junkies. If you don't believe me, put my theory to the test and watch how fast you get smoked.

<u>Time</u>

Attention and time go hand in hand, so there's no need for me to go hard on this subject. I'll start by saying this:

You can always make money, but you can never get your time back.

Just like spending money, you must spend time together for your union to succeed. Have you ever tried to get some "me time" in your relationship? How did that turn out for you? The person who "loves" you probably threw a hissy fit and gaslit you into feeling bad for wanting some personal space. Your free time is not your own, and an insecure partner will manipulate you into spending all of your time with them. If you dare give them some pushback or resistance, prepare yourself to be guilted and shamed into submission. By now, some of you are probably in shock by the things I've said in this book. Well, you should be. The wisdom I'm giving you is something you will never learn in school. This is the type of knowledge your Father was too afraid to tell you. I've experienced the guilt of wanting to spend some time alone in my past relationships. It's mentally draining. Try to take some "you time" one day in your relationship and watch what happens. That unconditional love will go up in flames faster than a spruce tree on a hot summer day.

Love is a temporary and fleeting emotion. It's nothing more than a mixture of lust and dopamine. Take a good look at the person you're with right now. There's a good chance you and that individual won't even be together in seven years. Every relationship has specific conditions that must be met. If those conditions aren't met, the love will cease and the engagement will be terminated. The only successful relationship is where the two people stay together forever. **This is true monogamy.**

Most of you don't practice monogamy. You guys practice "hot racking." This means you go from one person's bed to another, claiming to love each one in the process. You don't love those people. You're just practicing temporary sexual exclusivity with them.

Fidelity

I've been dreading writing this part since the start of my book, but I'm not going to tell lies on paper, so I'm going to keep it real here. If you cheat on your partner, you're a dirtbag. I've cheated in my past, which makes me a dirtbag. This part of the list is a no-brainer. If you're unfaithful in your relationship, you don't deserve to be loved. I think this is something we all can agree on. Infidelity should be an instant deal breaker, and no one deserves to be stepped out on.

Okay, ladies and gentlemen, let me just say this. I'm not telling you to completely avoid romance and be a hermit. I'm telling you to put yourself first and don't make love a priority.

You've got the rest of your life to be tied down. There's no need to rush.

Don't let romance movies and R&B music program you into finding a soulmate. Life is not a fairy tale or a Disney movie. Some of the most broken people dedicate their lives to love, and they're still unhappy. *Start by loving yourself first.* You are the most important person in your life. Remember that.

Before you decide to settle down, get a piece of paper and write down all of your goals and dreams. I want you to create a bucket list of all the things you'd like to do in your life. Don't commit to anyone until you've completed everything on your vision board. Listen to what I'm saying! No one in your social circle is going to tell you this, because they are slaves in an unfulfilling relationship. Remember this, my friends:

You come first.
Romance comes dead last.

You've got the rest of your life to be tied down to some man or woman. You'll find someone in time, but focus on yourself first. A lot of people will read this book and be disgusted with how I feel. Well, guess what? I don't care. I know that what I'm sharing is valuable knowledge, and I will stand by what I believe until the very end. You can call me every name in the book, but you can't call me a liar.

Keep this in mind:

Misery loves company. There are plenty of people out there in bad relationships, ready to sabotage the path you're on. This will ultimately lead you to your destruction. Do not let these hopeless people alter your life. You are the master of your destiny!

INTERMISSION #3

The world needs voices like mine because it's different from the masses.

CHAPTER 18
NOT BELIEVE IN YOURSELF

Why do you doubt yourself so much?

I know things have been kind of heavy lately, so I'm going to lighten the mood. I'm not all doom and gloom! All right, so let me start by saying this:

We all question ourselves and our abilities every day.

It's perfectly normal to be uncertain at times, but why are we like this? Is it because of the failures of our past? Or is it because we don't have faith in ourselves? In my experience, I've come to learn that past failures and lack of confidence in oneself lead to self-doubt. It's completely normal to be hesitant and unsure at times, but we must not allow those negative emotions to overpower us. I'll use myself as an example.

I've failed at many things in my life. This is no secret. To be honest, there's a lot of stuff I don't believe in anymore.

By now, you all know exactly where I stand regarding the beaten path. I choose *not* to put all my trust in others. I've learned to lean on myself and draw upon my strength. These are my affirmations:

I believe in myself and I love myself. I'm confident in who I am, and I'm my own biggest fan. I'm the most important person in my life, and I have complete faith in my abilities. My wellbeing comes first.

I understand that this sounds selfish, but I don't care. There aren't many people out there who have the balls to say what I just said. There's a negative stigma on putting yourself first, but that doesn't matter to me. Never feel bad for making yourself a priority. This is my life, and I'm the master of my fate. The choices I make will determine the outcome of my future. I choose myself.

Some may call me arrogant.
Well, I call them lost causes.

Never downplay yourself or what you're capable of. Keep your spirits high and don't let self-doubt slow you down. *I'm not going to sit here and tell you "feel good" stuff.* We all know our strong points and limitations. It's up to *you* to use the cards you've been dealt and turn them into success. Only you can figure that out. You will fall and want to quit, but you need to get your ass back up.

The journey ahead will be brutal, but you will never get anywhere if you don't have confidence in yourself.

The first step of the voyage starts with believing you can do whatever you set out to do

CHAPTER 19

BE AFRAID TO PRODUCE YOUR CONTENT

*Your biggest trolls will be
people you know.*

STOP what you're doing right now and ask yourself these two questions:

- If I wanted to produce content, would my significant other support me?
- If I wanted to start creating, would my family and friends have my back?

If you have a desire to bring your creations to life, do it. Don't hesitate or procrastinate. But beware of the ones closest to you. They will see you trying to make it and tear you down out of sheer jealousy.

Creating content is *making something*. It can be a book, art, poetry, dance, music, or a podcast. When it comes to being a producer, the sky's the limit. Content creation is not limited to the examples I just listed. It can be anything, as long as you're bringing your ideas to LIFE!

Most people are consumers. These people just consume media and are programmed NPCs.

Only a small portion of people are producers. These types of people are breathing life into their ideas.

I'm a producer.

I'm writing a book, and I'll have a podcast in the future. Most people never manifest their ideas onto paper or into some form of media, so I can say with extreme confidence that I'm one thousand steps ahead of most people. While some folks are binge-watching NETFLIX (consumption), I'm diligently working on my book and my podcast studio (producing).

There's a difference.

And if anyone wants to challenge me on what I just said, bring it on. All I need to ask you is this:

What have you created lately?

You have to be fierce when you begin to walk this path. I believe that everyone reading this right now is capable of producing something. It doesn't even have to be extravagant! It can be something as small as a poem. Anything you make with your talent and skill is content. However, you need to prepare yourselves to be roasted by the peanut gallery. There will always be someone who will critique your work. I recently experienced this from someone I've known for years. This person said this to me, and I quote:

**"I feel sorry for your readers.
They are only getting the partial truth."**

Let's take some time to analyze this statement.

For starters, everyone has the right to their own opinion, so I'm not mad at him or her for saying this. I'm appreciative of the negative criticism.

Second, there's no reason for this individual to feel sorry for you guys. My dear reader, you are choosing to read this content. You don't have to stick around! You're free to go whenever you please. By now, you all know that this book has been extremely controversial. For those of you still around, shout out to you. It's been a crazy ride, but we're almost finished.

Lastly, I've taken responsibility throughout my book. I don't need to lie about my life to sell my work.

When you decide to start producing content, I want you to observe how your friends and family react. If you get negative feedback from these people, it will discourage you from being a creator. I say let the negativity *push you* to bring your content to *life*. I want you all to rise above the nonsense and continue perfecting your craft. No matter what it is, create your content and take pride in your work.

Never be afraid to bring your ideas to life.

THE DREAM

In the summer of 2022, I had a terrible dream that shook me to my core. In this dream, I was facing twenty years of prison for a bad decision I'd made. I ended up taking a plea bargain, which reduced my sentence to eight years. My lawyer handed me my legal papers to fill out and said this:

"Sign these papers and then you'll go straight to jail."

This experience was vivid and it felt so real. When I woke up, I was grateful to realize I was only dreaming. Can you imagine being locked up? How would you react if you knew you were about to be incarcerated?

I want you to imagine putting your entire life on hold for eight years. Think about all of your hopes, goals, and dreams on pause for multiple years.

Do you honestly think that your family and friends are going to be there for you while you're in prison? People will barely contact you in the free world. What makes you think they'll keep in touch while you're in the pen? I want you to imagine all of your rights being taken away. Imagine being in a hostile and hateful environment with your state's worst offenders. Imagine living in a cold, filthy small cell in a pod full of angry inmates. What are you going to do when it's time to shower?

The shower is a hot spot for inmates to be stabbed. Whether you're gang-affiliated or not, every inmate is a potential target.

Who's going to protect you when you're vulnerable? Prison food is disgusting and commissary is a privilege, not a right. Don't even get me started on the correctional officers. Not only do you have to deal with the inmates, but you have to deal with the COs as well. Most of these guys are full of hatred, and they're going to make your life a living hell. Keeping in contact with your loved ones in the outside world will be chaotic. Good luck getting your friends and family to write to you or put money on your books. Also, there are only two phones in the dayroom. If you don't have rank, you may have to pay the inmates commissary just to use the phone! Not to mention, buying phone time is expensive, and the inmates may extort you for the time you've bought. Prison is hell on Earth. Every aspect of your life is micromanaged, and you're at the mercy of the inmates and staff.

FUCK THAT SHIT.

I was a correctional officer for three years, and it was an absolute nightmare. I was never locked up, but working in a prison showed me exactly why my dumb ass needs to stay on the straight and narrow! There's nothing cool about being in the penitentiary. You're only one bad choice away from a lifetime of regret.

It's imperative that we not only govern ourselves but that we're selective of our social element. This means that we must be cautious of who we associate and hang around with.

We must never put ourselves in a position to become slaves of the state. Never allow yourself to be at the mercy of the justice system. Your freedom is valuable, so appreciate it. You never know how much you miss something until it's gone. I know a lot of inmates who would do anything for a second chance. Don't be the person staring out a small metal window wishing to be on the outside again. I know some guys who are never coming home. It's not worth it.

This dream spoke to my mind, body, and spirit. I'm responsible for my actions and the choices I make. Whether you succeed in life or fail, you have no one else to blame but yourself.

CHAPTER 20

MAKING EXCUSES

Some people have all the answers.

I don't make excuses.
I make results.

Some people have an excuse for everything. They always have a reason or an explanation for their flaws and shortcomings. One of my biggest pet peeves is a person who always has a "one up" for everything. They're never wrong. Even when they're proven to be at fault, they still won't own up to it. These people are narcissists. You must keep an eye on characters like this. **They are manipulative and will always blame everything on someone else.**

I once dated a woman just like this. She was a gaslighter, a manipulator, and a professional victim. She was never wrong. Even when she was caught messing up, she wouldn't apologize. She'd just strawman me and say,

"Oh, like you've never done this before." It was life-draining and the main reason we broke up. I'm grateful that I don't have to deal with this individual anymore. **These types of mind games are witchcraft and sorcery.**

In my opinion, I think that women tend to excel in the world of psychological warfare. It's these passive-aggressive mind games combined with constant excuses that truly make someone toxic.

Women, if you want to keep a man, learn how to ***take responsibility for your actions and apologize.*** *We men have to endure being wrong every day. If we can do it, so can you. After all, hasn't feminism taught you that you can do anything a man can do?*

Men, this goes for you too. Stop being weak and man up when you mess up! You're better than making excuses.

We all need to boss up when we mess up.

Sometimes saying, "Hey, I screwed up; I'm sorry" is all a person needs to hear.

You'll never gain respect by making excuses.

But there's honor in taking responsibility.

CHAPTER 21

TELL PEOPLE THINGS THEY SHOULD NEVER DO

Did this topic of discussion surprise you?

It takes a crazy person to write an entire book just to contradict himself at the end. Nevertheless, there's a method to my madness. I'll gladly explain why I chose to end it this way.

This book is not meant to be "self-help" or an instructional manual.

This book is my story, and only I can tell it.

- I've made thirty revolutions around the sun.
- I have military experience (USMC) (VMA-542) (2011–2015) (Semper Fi).
- I battled some of my state's worst offenders as a correctional officer.

- I've lost many friends and family members due to how I think.
- I've been reborn as a new man, and I have a non-linear outlook on life.

Even with all of my experience, I still have much to learn, and I humbly accept that. As I've moved through life, I've noticed that people don't like being told what to do.

I don't like being told what to do either.

However, I'm man enough to admit it and own up to it. Generally, most people hate unsolicited advice. A lot of folks won't ask for mentorship until it's too late. You can lead a horse to water, but you can't make him drink. An individual can't be helped if they don't want to be helped.

Counseling someone gently will cause you problems. Laying down the hammer on someone will cause you problems.

You just can't win! But this is not about winning. Sometimes you just need to say your piece and keep it moving. In today's misguided and foolish society, don't waste your time telling people things they should never do. Most likely, it's going to fall on deaf ears. You can't tell a grown person what to do. People are going to make their own decisions, even if what they're doing is stupid.

Most people are oxygen thieves at best. They're a burden to society and parasites that absorb taxpayer dollars. Don't waste your time helping someone who doesn't help themselves.

Make people earn your wisdom.
Make them earn your time.

Coach those who want to be coached, and lead those who want to be taught.

You are worth more than being ignored. Just make sure you're strong in your beliefs before you go and start telling people ...

Things they should never do in their life.

BONUS

CHAPTER 22

NOT SHOWING LOVE TO THE PEOPLE!

For those of you who made it to the end, I want to thank you from the bottom of my heart. I know this was an intense ride. It takes guts to endure content that may rub you the wrong way. Shout out to everyone who agrees or disagrees with me. If it wasn't for you, I wouldn't have been able to share my story.

BONUS BONUS

CHAPTER 23
LEAVE YOUR READERS IN THE DARK

Currently, I'm building a podcast studio. I plan on writing a second and a third book in the future. I'd like to have a trilogy to my name someday.

My dream is to retire and move to Chiang Mai, Thailand in twenty years.

THE LAST ENTRY

This will be the final piece of my book.

When I was addicted to alcohol, I used to envy people who had successfully quit drinking. In my eyes, they were courageous and strong. I spent many years wishing I could quit too. On August 1, 2022, I decided to fly out to Las Vegas and celebrate my thirty-first birthday. It's been a blast out here these past few days! Unfortunately, this place gets stale quickly if you don't drink or gamble. When I was on Fremont Street, I decided to make a mad dash for The Mob Museum. The facility played a segment on The Prohibition Act of 1919, and it got me thinking about drinking again. Once more, I began to struggle. So I decided to reach out to a good friend of mine for some support.

I want you to imagine a former alcoholic being in sin city surrounded by vices of all types.

For eleven years, my greatest enemy was alcohol. My love for the bottle is the reason I walked away from it. Every part of me was screaming to drink again. When I told my friend I was going through it, he told me this:

"We all have our vices! Don't come back to booze. You aren't missing anything. It's easy to succumb in a place like Vegas. If you can hold out there, you can do it anywhere."

Douglas, you are my hero. I will remember those words for the rest of my life.

I never want to be in a position where I'm not in control. I will never go back to who I used to be.

21 Things You Should Never Do in Your LIFE

REFERENCES

Liedtke, Micheal. "Netflix loses 200,000 subscribers, projects even deeper losses this spring." *PBS*, 20 April 2022, https://www.pbs.org/newshour/arts/netflix-loses-200000-subscribers-projects-even-deeper-losses-this-spring#:~:text=Netflix%20loses%20200%2C000%20subscribers%2C%20projects%20even%20deeper%20losses%20this%20spring,-Arts%20Apr%2020&text=SAN%20FRANCISCO%20(AP)%20%E2%80%94%20Netflix,already%20seen%20its%20best%20days.

"Divorce Statistics: Over 115 studies, facts and rates for 2022." *Wikinson and Finkbeiner,* https://www.wf-lawyers.com/divorce-statistics-and-facts/

Robinson, Gary. "6 Reasons Why Women Are More Likely To File For Divorce Than Men." *DivorceMag.com,* 29 July 2021, https://www.divorcemag.com/blog/6-reasons-why-women-are-more-likely-to-file-for-divorce-than-men

BOOK DESCRIPTION

Pain, suffering, doubt, regret, suicidal thoughts, legal issues, financial issues, tattered friendships, destroyed relationships, emptiness, loneliness, redemption, and hope. This is a true story about how one man lost everything but ultimately gained his freedom.

21 Things is a non-conventional path for you to consider following if you're willing to challenge societal norms. Have you ever considered questioning God and Christianity? What about your family and friends? Do you believe in unconditional romantic love? *21 Things* is an authentic and brutally honest assessment of life and the people surrounding us.

Are you brave enough to walk outside the beaten path? There is no greater form of power than changing the laws in your mind and thinking for yourself.

AUTHOR BIO

Tracy Mills is a United States Marines Corps veteran (2011–2015). He was honorably discharged in 2015 and then went to serve as a correctional officer from 2015–2018. He now serves as a letter carrier. He has aspirations to create a YouTube channel and to become a content creator. He dreams of helping people on his own podcast through education and entertainment.

www.ingramcontent.com/pod-product-compliance
Lightning Source LLC
LaVergne TN
LVHW041640060526
838200LV00040B/1645